Browse our YouTube channel and check out the documentation of the *Invocation* #2.

Ministry of Culture, Government of the State of São Paulo,
through the Secretariat of Culture, Creative Economy and Industry,
Municipal Secretariat of Culture and Creative Economy of the City
of São Paulo, Fundação Bienal de São Paulo and Itaú present

Not All Travellers Walk Roads

36th Bienal de São Paulo

Of Humanity as Practice

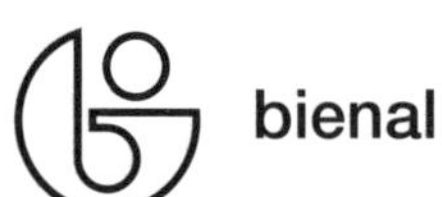

**Educational
Publication**

Vol. 2

*Bigidi mè
pa tonbé!*

Totter but
Never Fall!

Since 1953, the year of its second edition, the Bienal de São Paulo has stood out for its educational commitment, promoting initiatives that facilitate access to exhibition content for diverse audiences – including teachers, students, and educators. In 2009, the Fundação Bienal established a permanent education team that has since been developing and implementing educational projects for each edition. These projects include publications, guided visits, workshops, and training programs for teachers and educators, all aimed at fulfilling the Fundação Bienal's mission of expanding access to contemporary art.

For the 36th Bienal de São Paulo – *Not All Travellers Walk Roads – Of Humanity as Practice*, the Fundação presents a series of four educational publications with two complementary objectives, both of fundamental importance to the Bienal. The first is to document and share the contributions of the *Invocations* – curatorial gatherings with artists and poets that explore notions of humanity, the exhibition's central theme, through the lens of four distinct geographies: Marrakech, Guadeloupe, Zanzibar, and Tokyo. The second objective is to support the educational project of the 36th Bienal, with these books serving as key resources in the training of mediators and in outreach activities, both during the months of preparation and execution of the exhibition and throughout the traveling exhibitions program that will follow.

As is characteristic of the Bienal de São Paulo, the content of these publications weaves together local and global perspectives, addressing contemporary practices and issues. The result of a partnership with the Center for Art, Research and Alliances (CARA), which co-published the books with the Fundação Bienal, and the A&L Berg Foundation, which supported the project from the outset, these educational publications are now available in English and will be distributed internationally for the first time, expanding the reach of the *Invocations* and our educational content, and reaffirming the Bienal's international vocation, which has been continuously enacted for over seventy years.

Andrea Pinheiro
President – Fundação Bienal de São Paulo

CARA is thrilled to co-produce this publication with the Bienal de São Paulo, reinforcing our shared commitment to expanding spaces for artistic and intellectual inquiry. The *Invocations* programs and these four educational volumes echo CARA's dedication to publishing as an act of transformation – where knowledge is not just recorded but activated through encounters across disciplines and geographies. Our institutional approach fosters open-ended research, challenges fixed narratives, and embraces storytelling as a means of keeping ideas in motion, unsettling dominant histories, and opening pathways for unlearning.

Building on this ethos, CARA's publishing program amplifies overlooked voices, supporting elder and mid-career practitioners and alternative historiographies. Our books embrace literary and poetic practices; visual, moving-image, and performance art; and radical action as entangled forces shaping how we understand our interconnected worlds. Through the *Invocations* series, CARA furthers its commitment to publishing as a space of resonance – where artistic and intellectual work resists singular narratives. This collaboration with the 36th Bienal de São Paulo strengthens our mission to amplify artists, scholars, and cultural workers whose contributions shape critical discourse, foster new connections, and expand the boundaries of thought.

At CARA, we ask: How can we dream not only about ourselves? This question guides our editorial vision, inviting us to create spaces where knowledge is shared and deepened in dynamic relation. For us, publishing is a process of bringing into generative constellation – where voices converge, entangle, and expand what can be imagined together. This collaboration embodies that ethos, offering books that challenge, unsettle, and inspire new ways of thinking and being in the world.

Manuela Moscoso
Executive and Artistic Director – CARA

The A&L Berg Foundation, founded in 2023 by Allison and Larry Berg, provides access, tools and resources to create, evolve and sustain diverse perspectives and narratives in the United States visual arts. We support and empower individuals committed to making systemic and scalable impact in their practices and communities.

The Foundation's core program is the ESAP Fellowship, which supports and empowers early stage visual arts curators, educators and administrators working in United States arts spaces and institutions. Through building a long-lasting peer support system, and providing navigational tools and opportunities to create expanded professional networks and communities, the Foundation creates equitable visual arts career pathways and ultimately aims to strengthen and diversify the internal ecosystems of United States art institutions.

Our programs provide access to networks, professional development workshops, international research travel, mentorship, relational and soft skills coaching, and financial support for navigating systemic inequities. Each year, a different jury of esteemed arts professionals nominates candidates based on an agreed upon set of criteria, and we invite six of those individuals to participate in the fellowship cohort. Our guest program director, an arts professional who has already successfully navigated the challenges facing the respective cohort, designs the annual program details with a focus on the relational skills that specific cohort requires for career growth.

During the ten-month fellowship, the Foundation provides five empowerment prongs: mentorship with a more established arts professional; relational skills workshops with specialists spanning a variety of industries; an unrestricted financial grant; a robust international research trip opening doors and offering engagement with visual art leaders and peers from every part of the global art ecosystem and ongoing support for professional growth.

A&L Berg Foundation

The Fundação Bienal de São Paulo thanks its partners CARA and A&L Berg Foundation for their special collaboration on the educational publications of the 36th Bienal.

The Federal Government, through the Ministry of Culture, is celebrating the 36th Bienal de São Paulo in partnership with the Fundação Bienal de São Paulo. Just like the great film festivals, the Bienal de São Paulo – the second oldest art biennial in the world – raises enormous expectations on the global exhibition circuit. This year, with the title *Not All Travellers Walk Roads – Of Humanity as Practice*, inspired by a poem by the renowned Brazilian writer Conceição Evaristo, the Bienal reaffirms its vocation as a major showcase for the most current production on the national and global art scene, without losing sight of its wide-ranging educational activities in the formation of new and well-known audiences.

The Ministry of Culture has been working to strengthen the cultural sector through various initiatives and promotion tools. Policies such as the Paulo Gustavo Law and the Aldir Blanc National Policy for the Promotion of Culture encourage other artistic languages, creating opportunities for artists, cultural producers, managers, and visitors. Creating solid conditions for culture means strengthening the creative economy and encouraging the implementation of perennial, permanent, and democratic cultural policies.

Being alongside projects like the Bienal's new movie theater is a source of pride, as it brings together two issues dear to the government: expanding democratic access to cultural facilities combined with an educational arm capable of mediating and making sense of what is on display. By providing free film screenings accompanied by educational activities, another stage is created to strengthen the culture of our country's award-winning and increasingly active audiovisual field.

The Federal Government remains committed to arts and education, which are indispensable fronts for ensuring the right to citizenship and a fairer future for all. We will continue to invest in initiatives that encourage cultural creation and innovation, ensuring that events such as the Bienal de São Paulo continue to inspire and transform generations.

Margareth Menezes
Minister of Culture – Federal Government of Brazil

For more than 35 years, Itaú Cultural (IC) has played a fundamental role in boosting the appreciation of art, culture and education in a complex and heterogeneous society like Brazil. This role is expanded through essential partners for the development of the cultural and creative economy, such as the Fundação Bienal de São Paulo.

Itaú Unibanco is proud to be a sponsor of the Fundação Bienal de São Paulo – it has been for the past 27 years, with this being the 12th edition held in that period – reaffirming its commitment to promoting the visual arts and their transformative role. The Bienal de São Paulo is an important meeting and exchange space for artists, curators, critics, and the public.

In this field, Itaú Cultural organizes actions for enjoyment, education and promotion, including solo and group exhibitions that take place both at its headquarters on Avenida Paulista, 149 (with free admission) and at venues in Brazil's five regions. Highlights of the 2025 exhibitions include *Carlos Zilio – A querela do Brasil*, curated by Paulo Miyada, which will present a retrospective of this artist who, with erudition and irreverence, explored the tensions of Brazilian art. Exhibitions will also be dedicated to the visual artist Rivane Neuenschwander and the curator and critic Paulo Herkenhoff.

Visit itaucultural.org.br to browse the *Filmes e vídeos de artistas* virtual exhibitions, with experimental audiovisual works, and *Livros de artista na Coleção Itaú Cultural*, whose immersive and interactive features allow for detailed appreciation. At Enciclopédia Itaú Cultural (enciclopedia. itaucultural.org.br) you can access hundreds of entries on figures, works, and events in the visual arts.

Being present at the Bienal de São Paulo reinforces our goal of building links with different audiences, valuing the diversity of formats, thoughts, and subjectivities, and fostering creative and critical thinking through Brazilian art and culture.

Itaú Cultural

Bloomberg is proud to sponsor of the 36th edition of the Bienal de São Paulo. For more than a decade we have supported the Bienal's exceptional contemporary art exhibitions in the stunning Ciccillo Matarazzo Pavilion in Ibirapuera Park and around Brazil, through our partnership with Fundação Bienal. This year's edition continues the tradition of presenting captivating and thought-provoking art installations that are free and open to the public.

Every day, Bloomberg connects influential decision makers to a dynamic network of information, people, and ideas. With more than 19,000 employees in 176 offices, Bloomberg delivers business and financial information, news and insight around the world. Our dedication to innovation and new ideas extends to our longstanding support of arts, which we believe are a valuable way to engage citizens and strengthen communities. Through our funding, we help increase access to culture and empower artists and cultural organizations to reach broader audiences.

Bloomberg

For Bradesco, a Brazilian bank *par excellence* that has just celebrated its 83rd anniversary, art and culture are not only fundamental elements in the formation of a people's identity or the construction of their intangible heritage, but also a journey of inclusion and citizenship, a healthy convergence of different points of view. It is, so to speak, a journey towards the new, but with the care to value what is special enough to be history or tradition.

Therefore, when it comes to art and culture, the boundaries between past, present, and future, between form and content, become meaningless. Everything becomes reflection and learning, everything becomes provocation and surprise.

It was on the basis of this interpretation, combined with the positive view of the role of companies in making possible what society considers important, that Bradesco became a sponsor of the 36th edition of the Bienal de São Paulo, undoubtedly one of the most important events in the country aimed at promoting the arts scene, publicizing the various expressions of art and promoting cultural exchange, with all the good that this brings.

By participating in something that is both great and multifaceted, Bradesco shares with the Fundação Bienal de São Paulo – which has organized the event for more than six decades – the goal of democratizing access to culture, multiplying its reach and promoting the appreciation of art.

It's a path with no end, no turning back, full of challenges and at least one certainty: the more people who take part, the better!

Bradesco

Petrobras has a history of more than forty years of continuously believing in culture as a transformational element and a source of energy for society. By supporting unique projects and long-term partnerships, we have built a relationship of respect and collaboration with producers and initiatives all over the country.

The Petrobras Cultural Program has Brazilianness as its guiding element, which is materialized in the themes, origins, curatorship, history, and characteristics of each project we select. By supporting different projects, we put into practice our belief that culture is an important energy that transforms society. We believe that through creativity and inspiration we promote growth and change.

The Bienal de São Paulo is one of the sector's most prestigious events in the country and the world. Petrobras's sponsorship reinforces the company's role in promoting culture in its various forms, consolidating its position as one of the biggest supporters of the arts in Brazil.

Events such as the Bienal de São Paulo make a significant contribution to the economy, promoting innovation, creativity, and sustainability in the economic dynamic. Petrobras is an ally of Brazil's development in its various sectors. It invests in many forms of energy, and culture is certainly one of them.

Petrobras is proud to support Brazilian culture in its plurality of manifestations, taking art to all audiences, all over the country. Because culture is also our energy.

To find out more about the Petrobras Cultural Program, visit petrobras.com.br/cultura.

Petrobras

Instituto Vale Cultural believes in the transformative power of culture. As one of the main supporters of culture in Brazil, it sponsors and promotes projects that foster connections between people, initiatives, and territories. Its commitment is to make culture increasingly accessible and diverse, while also contributing to the strengthening of the creative economy.

It is therefore a pleasure to be part of the realization of this 36th Bienal de São Paulo and its educational program, which explores new formats and approaches. Developed from the *Invocations* proposed by the curatorial team – encounters with poetry, music, performance, and debates that explore notions of humanity across different geographies – the educational program expands the Bienal's communication with diverse audiences and extends its reach beyond the exhibition space and timeframe, in an interdisciplinary way.

With each new edition, the Bienal invites us to rethink art as an exercise in dialogue, in openness to new narratives, and as a space for learning. In this sense, it aligns with the purpose of the Instituto Cultural Vale: to expand opportunities for learning, reflection, new perspectives, and the sharing of art, culture, and education – both inside and outside museums, throughout Brazil.

Where there is culture, Vale is there

Instituto Cultural Vale

For 110 years, Citi has been part of Brazil's history, accompanying its transformations and driving its development. Our journey is intertwined with that of the country: we are both witnesses to and participants in a Brazil that constantly reinvents itself and moves forward.

More than a financial institution, we believe in the power of culture and education as engines for a more inclusive, innovative, and sustainable future. Investing in these pillars also means celebrating the diversity, creativity, and talent that define the Brazilian spirit.

With this commitment, we are proud, for the first time, to support the 36th Bienal de São Paulo – one of the most important spaces for artistic expression in Latin America, where Brazil thinks, feels, and reinvents itself through art.

We believe in art as an agent of social transformation. Artistic creation has the power to spark dialogue, expand horizons, and inspire new possibilities for the world. By sponsoring the Bienal, we reaffirm our commitment to culture, innovation, and all those who, through art, are building new narratives for both the present and the future.

Citi

Vivo believes in culture as a means of social transformation and is one of the most important brands supporting the visual and performing arts and music in Brazil. Art, like technology, creates connections between people and encourages the search for balance between history, nature and time.

Vivo is currently a sponsor of the most important museums in Brazil, such as the Museu de Arte de São Paulo Assis Chateaubriand (MASP), the Pinacoteca de São Paulo, the Museu da Imagem e do Som (MIS-São Paulo), the Museu Afro Brasil Emanoel Araujo, the Museu de Arte Moderna de São Paulo (MAM SP), as well as the Instituto Inhotim and the Palácio das Artes, both in Minas Gerais, and the Museu Oscar Niemeyer, in Paraná.

Teatro Vivo, located in São Paulo, offers a curated selection of contemporary plays that promote reflection on current issues and value cultural diversity. In addition, it is a fully accessible space, offering resources such as translation into Libras (Brazilian sign language), audio descriptions and trained staff, ensuring inclusion for people with disabilities and reduced mobility. In 2024, it welcomed over 50,000 people.

The brand also supports projects in the world of music that are genuinely Brazilian and regional, reinforcing its proximity with local culture at iconic and traditional events in our country, such as the Parintins Festival, Galo da Madrugada, the Çairé Festival, Lollapalooza, The Town, and Vivo Música.

The brand's initiatives in the cultural sphere broaden access to knowledge with new ways of experiencing and learning, strengthened by the aspects of diversity, sustainability, inclusion and education. All information is gathered and shared on the @vivo.cultura and @vivo Instagram profiles.

Vivo

Confronted with the incessant problems of humanity, perhaps it is worth dwelling a little longer on some open questions, taking sustenance from resources that allow us to dig and build answers procedurally. In this sense, art, in its many guises, offers fertile ground for critical elaborations about the world and ourselves.

The meeting of art and education – both understood as fields of knowledge – enables the torsion of time and space: it becomes possible, thus, to suspend neutralities and dilate what is precipitated in structures. How far is this approach able to infer the real and interfere in it? It allows us to (re)populate imaginaries, to unpick the universalizing statute attributed to concepts, practices and people, and thus to carve out reality with narratives that articulate the individual and the collective, in a procedural and coherent manner regarding the issues that permeate existence.

It is according to this panorama that Sesc São Paulo and the Fundação Bienal, through the 35th Bienal de São Paulo, reiterate their long-standing partnership, a mutual commitment to fostering experiences of coexistence with the visual arts, expanding access to cultural actions and the exercise of otherness.

This partnership, which has been established and renewed for over a decade, has led to the promotion of projects such as simultaneous exhibitions, public meetings, seminars and training for educators, as well as the consolidated itinerant exhibition with excerpts from the Bienal in Sesc units in the wider state of São Paulo. The confluence of choices and propositions is part of the institutional perspective of culture as a right, and conceives, together with one of the largest exhibitions in the country, an accessible horizon for contemporary art in Brazil.

Sesc São Paulo

Foreword
Fundação Bienal de São Paulo

This book is an extension of the investigations into notions of humanity in different parts of the world, engaging with the ideas of the 36th Bienal de São Paulo – *Not All Travellers Walk Roads – Of Humanity as Practice* from the second *Invocation – Bigidi mè pa tonbé!* [Totter, but never fall!] –, which took place in Les Abymes, Guadeloupe, in December 2024.

The *Invocations* are meetings with presentations of poetry, research, music, and dance that preceded the exhibition in São Paulo. In addition to Guadeloupe, they also took place in three other territories: Marrakech in November 2024, Zanzibar and Tokyo in February and April 2025, respectively.

In her oral work *Ôrí*,[1] the historian Beatriz Nascimento points out that "Memory is the contents of a continent, its life, its history, its past. As if the body were the document." Under these words, we begin down the paths of this second volume of the 36th Bienal's educational publication, revealing ways of existing and resisting, in the encounter between the reflections proposed by *Invocation* #2 and those of Brazilian thinkers in the face of manifestations that draw attention to this pulsating archive that is the body.

"It's no wonder that, for Black people, dancing is a foundation for liberation," says Nascimento. As professor Leda Maria Martins explains in her poetics of the body-screen, dance manifests a knowledge written on the body, a heritage,[2] while anthropologist Marlene Cunha uses Candomblé poses – *gincado, adobá, barravento* and *arrebate*[3] – to establish an ethnography of gesture. A companion in Beatriz Nascimento's struggle, Cunha's gaze turns to religions of African origin in Brazil in the 1980s, seeking, above all, to recognize an ethos in the ritual, its reflexes in everyday life, and its contributions to establishing a culture of resistance.[4]

Invocation #2 was centered on the reflections of teacher and choreographer Léna Blou, who identifies in the concept of *Bigidi*[5] the essence of the Caribbean being, a symbol of their worldview and a strategy of resistance for acting on life.[6] In her text "The *Bigidi*, an a Knowledge Incarnate at the Heart of the *Lawonn*," Blou asks: "Why, in one place on Earth, do people dance in chaos?" The question resonates in movements that we can recognize across the more than 4,000 kilometers that separate Guadeloupe from Brazil. It is reminiscent of capoeira, candomblé, *samba de roda*, and other Afro-Brazilian dances, and chimes with another question posed by actress, dancer, and founder of the Afrofunk platform, Taísa Machado: "What kind of artist is the artist who develops in war?"[7]

A feint, a dodge, a temporal discontinuity, fluidity, a break: *Bigidi*. But contrary to what one might understand at first glance – or in the first gesture – *Bigidi* is not a summary of *Gwoka* – a cultural expression that combines liturgical songs in Guadeloupe Creole, dances and the sounds of drums called *ka*.[8] It is established in the *Gwoka* and extrapolates it, it takes place in an "in-between" of disorder [*Bigidi*] and adaptation [*Rèpriz*] in the circularity of the *Lawonn*,[9] also reflecting a social construction and perception that, at its foundation, rearticulates chaos, and turns imbalance into a tool for adaptability.

An Intangible Cultural Heritage of the state of Rio de Janeiro, the body of *Passinho*, which articulates the *sabará*, the *puxada*, the *laço*,[10] is an example that instigates reflection on this notion of balance and imbalance contained in *Bigidi*. "Through sound and body movement, the young group symbolically reworks space, insofar as it modifies, albeit momentarily, territorial hierarchies, stimulating the expressive power of the body to the point of producing its own images of liberation and self-realization," says Muniz Sodré.[11]

So we set off from here – Brazil – to begin structuring the dance that unfolds over the next few pages, moving towards what was happening there – Guadeloupe – in a crossing of repertoires mobilizing poetry, dance, performance, the body, languages, stories.

The artist Geordy Zodidat Alexis, in his *"Kalanjé,"* with his performative writing, points out that *Bigidi* is a way of life, a starting point and initiation for understanding the people of Caroucaera – Cibuqueira (Guadeloupe), the island where he was born. In *"An Sé,"* Dory Sélèsprika, a poet and slammer, together with Anaïs Verspan, a visual artist, mobilize a space-time for re-elaborating narratives, moving towards what Léna Blou points out about *Bigidi* and the relationships that unfold in language, landscape, and consciousness.

Poetic language is also present in this volume through the collaboration of the educator and poet Edinho Santos, whose poems, often used in different spaces as an educational tool, provoke an active and manifold reading experience. A dance between the balance and imbalance of the body that rhymes with Brazilian Sign Language – Libras. You can access Edinho's collaboration via QR Codes and, whether you know Libras or not, you can get closer to what he is sharing, either by translating the poems or by allowing yourself to engage in a dance-conversation: What does the body suggest? What does the gesture carry?

24 The participation of Yane Mareine, Minia Biabiany, and Santiago Quintana in the Guadeloupe *Invocation* is presented here as a record of words that dance between the poetic and the imagetic, providing insights into the body, gesture, presence, and time. The interconnectedness of relationships that echo in the body as a vehicle in the poetic text "Independence – Change – Living."

Feint, dodge, rupture, adaptation, balance, and imbalance all permeate the stories of Brazilian artist Lidia Lisbôa. Born in 1970 in Vila Guarani, Terra Roxa, Paraná, her narratives meet those of a multitude of people and are an invitation that entangles, from the wefts and knots of her textile works to the delicate grooves of the clay termite mounds.

After all, how do we keep our balance in motion in times of crisis? In dialogue with this, Michelle Mycoo calls us to action with an essay that reflects on the Earth as a living manifestation of the notions of balance and imbalance. Looking at the Caribbean islands, Mycoo reminds us that climate crises have no borders and reinforces the need for adaptation strategies ranging from green and blue infrastructure[12] to access to funding.

A collective call to action is also evoked by the *Blip*, a sound that is a space for the unpredictable. In the essay "The *Blip* and the *Pi Tak*: Humanity Verbs of the Improbable," Étienne Jean-Baptiste presents the onomatopoeia *Blip* and *Pi Tak* from an idea that transcends sound, symbolizing a grammar originating from the encounter with the imbalance generated by colonization, the "fractures of the New World."

The researcher Bruno Pinheiro looks at the Brazilian painter and composer Heitor dos Prazeres, who won third place for his work *Moenda* [Sugarcane Mill] at the 1st Bienal de São Paulo. Pinheiro dialogues with the self-portrait *Sonho* [Dream], made by him in the early years of his career as a visual artist, between 1938 and 1939. The relationships established in the text lead us to a dance between the balance and imbalance of representations that opposed stereotypes of Black bodies in 20th-century Brazil, which was shrouded in political and social tensions. What is the artist dreaming of? What dances do the waters that cover his sleep carry?

In this book you can also try out activities developed by the Fundação Bienal team in partnership with educators and teachers from different disciplines in formal and non-formal education. The proposals can be seen as tools to broaden discussions, based on the body, mobilizing gesture, listening, and circularity.

"We think with our body," says Bonaventure Soh Bejeng Ndikung, curator of the 36th Bienal de São Paulo, in his article.

25 His writing mobilizes the concept of corpoliteracy, which recognizes the body as a living space of memories, stories, acquisition, and the transmission of knowledge. From this, the text goes on to present the practice of storytelling as a foundation for existence, understanding the body – Corpoliteracy – as a repository of memories and narratives that can be activated and shared through movement, through dance.

We hope that, through the following pages, our bodies may dance, dance, and dance "until they are tired."

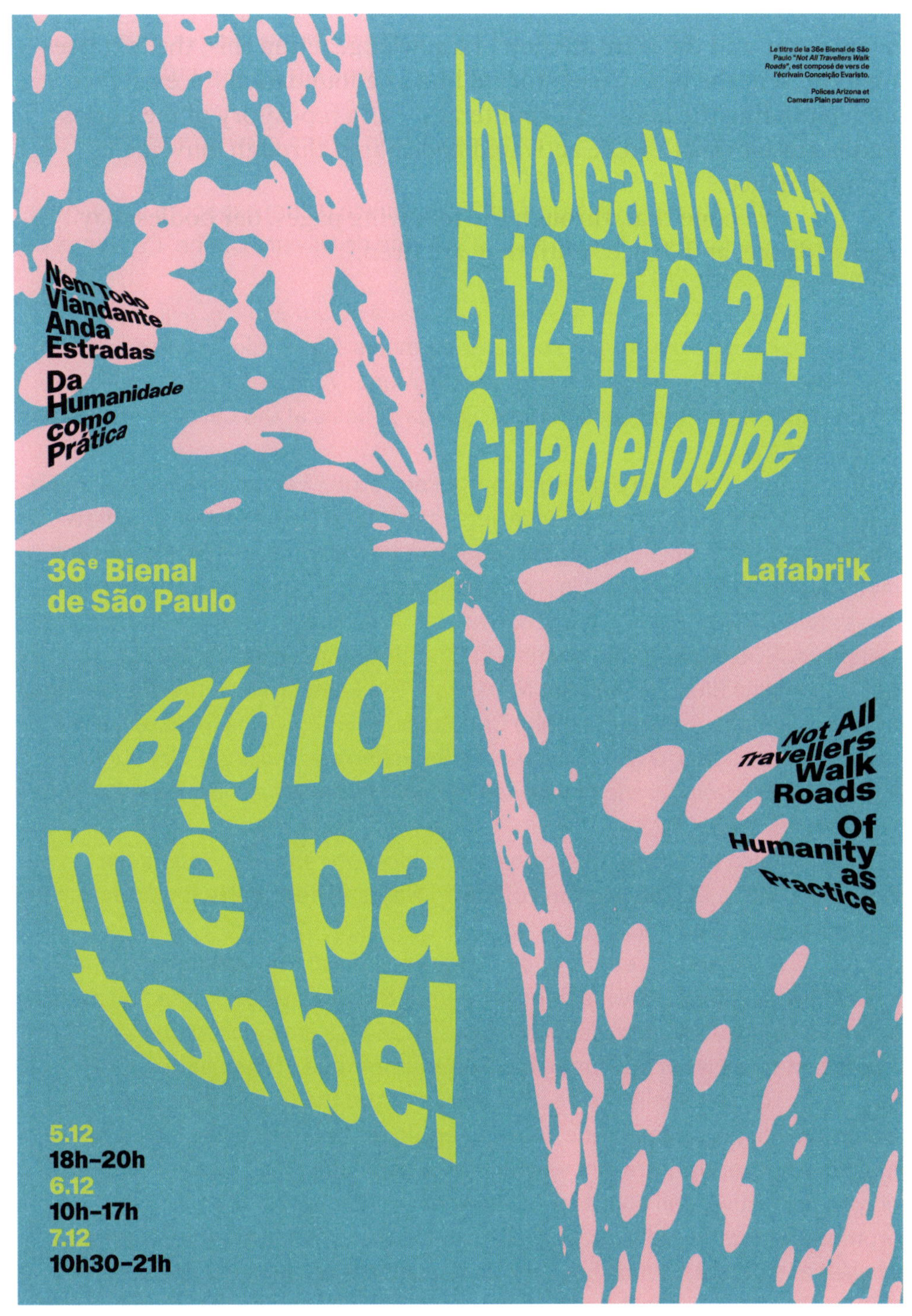

Poster for *Invocation #2*, December 5-7, 2024
© Studio Yukiko / Fundação Bienal de São Paulo

1   *Ôri* was documented in the film of the same name directed by Raquel Gerber. Brazil: Estelar Produções Cinematográficas e Culturais Ltda, 1989, video (131 min), color.

2   Leda Maria Martins, *Performances do tempo espiralar: poéticas do corpo-tela*. Rio de Janeiro: Cobogó, 2021.

3   João Alipio de Oliveira Cunha, Em busca de um espaço: a linguagem gestual no candomblé – À memória de Marlene de Oliveira Cunha. *Cadernos de Campo*. São Paulo: 2017.

4   Marlene de Oliveira Cunha, *Em busca de um espaço: a linguagem gestual no candomblé de Angola*. Master's thesis. São Paulo: Universidade de São Paulo, 1986. We would like to thank the Museu Afro Brasil Emanoel Araujo for the opportunity to access Marlene Cunha's thesis at the Carolina Maria de Jesus Library.

5   In her talk "Le *Bigidi*: une parole de l'être!," Léna Blou says that *Bigidi* is a magical word, capable of conveying its meaning even to those who have never heard the Creole language of Guadeloupe. According to Blou, the word materializes, in the body and in its pronunciation, the balanced-unbalanced movement – the stumbling that does not fall. Available at: www.youtube.com/watch?v=u8Oojo5pJqg&ab_channel=TEDxTalks>. Accessed on: 2025.

6   Léna Blou, "Totter, but Never Fall! The Feint of Time, the Wandering of the Body, and the Ambigidité of the Caribbean Being," in Olga Schubert and Eric Otieno Sumba (eds.), *O Quilombismo: Of Resisting and Insisting. Of Flight as Fight. Of Other Democratic Egalitarian Political Philosophies*. Berlin: Haus der Kulturen der Welt, 2023.

7   Taísa Machado, *O afrofunk e a ciência do rebolado*. São Paulo: Cobogó, 2020, p.18. The Afrofunk platform works to decolonize the body through dance and funk carioca.

8   Present in all ethnic and religious groups of the population of the island of Guadeloupe, *Gwoka* brings together these areas of expression as well as valuing individual improvisational skills. In 2014, it was placed on the Representative List of the Intangible Cultural Heritage of Humanity.

9   The *Lawonn* is the circular space where the *Gwoka* is danced and which aims to be a democratic, intergenerational, and inclusive place where all people, whoever they are, are welcome. For Léna Blou, the *Lawonn* would also play "a protective, unifying, and socializing role, because it is a place that promotes empathy, individual freedom, democracy, inclusion, acceptance of oneself and others, mutual help, solidarity, and the creation of improvisation." Still for the author, "it is the secure sociability of the *Lawonn* that allows the *Bigidi* to flourish for a necessary circularity."

10   *Passinho* is thought of here as a means of relating to different Afro-Brazilian popular dances. Although it was born on the outskirts of Rio de Janeiro, it spread throughout Brazil and even with variations in gestures, movements, and nomenclature, it continued to be fed by other body expressions. In addition, its existence can be seen as a strong aspect between balance and imbalance.

11	Muniz Sodré, "Cultura, corpo e afeto," *Dança: Revista do Programa de Pós-Graduação em Dança*, Salvador: UFBA, v.3, n.1, pp.18-19, 2014.

12	Green and blue infrastructure relates to strategies and interventions that use natural and sustainable elements to achieve environmental, social, and economic benefits in urban and rural spaces, integrating urban forestry/agriculture and water systems.

29

We Danced, Danced, Danced "Until We Were Tired": Further Reflections on Corpoliteracy

Bonaventure Soh Bejeng Ndikung

Reproduction of the opening speech
given on December 5, 2024.

We danced, danced,
Shaken our miseries to make our dreams shine,
struck the ground with all our strength
to make the waves of songs spring forth
The wind, in our hands, turned to dust.
Our joys in fireworks
lit up our sky.
And the aching feet, blowing at rest
Wondered about tomorrow's stage.
We danced, danced, danced "until tired."

From the poem "Nous avons dansé" [We danced], de Bernard Binlin Dadié[1]

Prelude

It is worth beginning with two disclaimers here.

While it is obvious for many of us, it might not be obvious for all that "until we tired" or "until we were tired" does not imply the literal tiredness. The tiredness here is comparable to the notion of bad when one says that a very good piece of music is "baddddd" with an elastic emphasis on the stretched "d," or when one says in a bout of deep laughter or deep joy that "I am deaddddd" with the "d" again carrying the weight of the expression. Which is to say the hyperbolized utterance of an antagonism to express a feeling. So "We danced, danced, danced until tired" seems to me a superlative of emotions that one can feel and emanate upon an elaborate and elaborated dance.

Then there is the nuanceness in the space of *"jusqu'à fatigué"*… "until we tired" or "until we were tired." In that space of translation the question of whether the helping verb "to be" is present or absent makes a world of a difference: between "we danced until we tired" and "we danced until we were tired" is a yawning gap that articulates something pertinent not about tiredness itself but the possibility of dance to act upon the outside as is the case with the former "we danced until we tired" and the possibility of dance to act upon the inside, which is the case with the latter "we danced until we were tired."

In the main concept of the 36th Bienal de São Paulo, we set a point of gravity in the space or context of storytelling. We intend to stage an art biennale as a concatenation of stories or storytelling sessions. It is worth bringing in Chinua Achebe here again, who in an interview for the New York State Writers Institute in 1998 was asked, "What is the importance of stories?" And he responded:

Well, it is story(telling) that makes us human. And that's why we insist. Whenever we are in doubt about who we are, we go to stories because this is one thing that we have done in the human race. There is no group that doesn't do it. It seems to be central to the very nature, to the very fact of our humanity to tell who we are. And to let that story keep us in mind of this. Because there will be days when we are not quite sure whether we are human or even more commonly whether other people are human with us. It is in the story that we get this continuity of this affirmation that you are human and that your humanity is contingent on the humanity of your neighbor.

Storytelling is foundational to our existence and is a core of our cosmogonies. So permit me to tell you two stories…

Act I: The Story of the Dancing Granny

Once upon a time, there was a Granny who not only loved to dance but was actually a formidable dancer. Whenever she heard music – and let's just say that, for her, even the sound of the pestle hitting the mortar was music – she couldn't help dancing. She danced all day and night while working, eating, conversing, gardening, and rumours went that she danced in her sleep. She even danced while she walked – to make reference here to Brother Abdourahman Waberi's formidable memoir with the title *Pourquoi tu danse quand tu marche?* [Why do you dance when you walk?]. When there was music she danced and when there was no music she would hum or sing herself into dancing. That is how she earned her most deserved pseudonym "the Dancing Granny."

The Dancing Granny was also a very gifted gardener and her plants grew lusciously, beautifully, colorfully and strongly from the energies and spirits of dancing she breathed into them.

On one blessed day, the good old Spider Ananse spotted the succulent vegetables growing in the Dancing Granny's garden. He knew fully well how much she loved dancing. So as Spider Ananse salivated upon the sight of the vegetables, he came up with a vicious plan to distract The Dancing Granny so as to be able to steal her vegetables. So Spider Ananse conjured the finest songs from afar, and the Dancing Granny carried away by the music danced away to the source of the music far away from her garden. When she returned in the evening, she found empty baskets as Spider Ananse had stolen all the beans she had harvested.

She swore to herself never to fall into Spider Ananse's music and dance trap again. But the next day, Spider Ananse came by, pulled the same trick and when she came back from her dancing spree in the evening, she found empty baskets of maize and groundnuts, as Spider Ananse had helped himself again.

The third day, Spider Ananse came singing the irresistible song, and in the blink of an eye, The Dancing Granny grabbed him and started dancing with him. Soon enough Spider Ananse was infected by Granny's groove and he too was whirling and twirling and never even thought of his kleptomanic tendencies.

When we were told this story over and over again as children, the centrality of dance in the narrative wasn't lost on us. Dance could make or break. It could be used or misused. But what was most important was the power it carried.

Because as children we woke up to dancing and went to bed dancing. In good times and bad. With or without food in our stomachs.

We danced not just for the sake of dancing but because dancing was an exercise of the body and mind, because through dancing we could express ourselves in ways that words cannot, because through dancing we learned and embodied knowledges and the codes of the outside world. It is through dancing that we made friends and learned how to navigate different kinds of terrains – literally and metaphorically.

Act II: The Story of the Dance for Water and the Rabbit

Once upon a time, a terrible drought befell our lands and the lakes, rivers, streams, ponds and springs went dry. Desperation was in the air as all the animals roamed around in search of water, but to no avail.

Then an emergency general assembly of animals was called. The elephant, lion, monkey and other animals proposed ideas but none seemed to befit the drastic environmental situation they were stuck in.

Then one of the animals came up with the idea that all the animals should go to the river bed and dance until water flows again. In their desperation, all the animals were ready to give this crazy idea a try, except the rabbit who just didn't believe this would work out.

So all the other animals went down to the river bed, and danced and danced and danced "until they tired," "until they were tired." And as they danced, water poured out to the surface and they could finally quench their thirst.

Because Sir Rabbit didn't contribute to the efforts to get water, the animal kingdom prohibited him from drinking from the source.

But being a trickster, Sir Rabbit wasn't going to follow that ban. So in the night he sneaked out to the river and drank to the fullness of his belly, and as if that was not enough, he had the guts to come back provoking the other animals and asking them how they intended to take out the water from his body.

The animals summoned another general assembly to deliberate on how to punish Sir Rabbit for his truancy and he was thereby levied the death sentence. Now the question was who was fast enough to catch the rabbit. Surprisingly, the old tortoise stepped forth and claimed that if there was anyone here smart enough to catch the rabbit then it was he.

Tortoise rubbed his shell with beeswax, went to the riverside and chilled waiting for the rabbit to come again in the night.

Sir Rabbit came, saw a stone on which he could stand to drink properly from the river. And as he climbed upon the stone, he got stuck in the beeswax on the old tortoise's shell.

When the tortoise brought the rabbit to the assembly of animals, the question was now how to execute the death penalty. Sir Rabbit was fast to propose that if he had to die he would at least like to choose his method of dying and thereby proposed that they should take him by the tail and dash his head against a stone.

As the lion executioner grabbed Sir Rabbit and swung him around several times to dash his head against a stone, the rabbit shed his fur and slipped out of the lion's paw to freedom.

Despite the fact that there are many morals to this narrative, it is actually only the first part of this story that is of interest to us in this context.

Dance had the power to end a drought. The possibility that dancing collectively could set the dry earth in vibration such that water could flow is something I find intriguing, especially, again, the inward and outward impact of dance.

It is obviously most unfortunate to bring in the dictum *cogito, ergo sum* [I think, therefore I am] from the 1637 *Discourse on the Method*, written by René Descartes, in this context, but since it serves as an ultimate reference for western philosophy, it is worth using it as a counterpoint to the essence of many non-Western, but especially African thought structures.

In our context, the notion of "I" makes sense only within the paradigm of the "I" and "I." The bigger "I" that can only be understood as the we. The collectivity of I's that make up society as a body larger than the individual. If one animal had danced at the bank of the river, there would most probably have been water. It was the collective of "I" that made the difference.

Maybe one of the biggest lies of Western universalist thought or propaganda has been to give us the impression that we are indivisible individuals. Which is to say the "I." While we have always been and will continue to be "dividuals," as our singular entities or units are only complete when they are part of the whole. We never think alone. Nor do we dream alone. We act, dream, think, dance, and live in relation. And our actions, dreams, thoughts, lives are contingent on the actions, dreams, thoughts, lives of our "neighbors" in the biblical sense of that word.

Act III: The Thinking Body

We think with our body. Our minds are embodied. Every cell, tissue, organ of the body is a thinking unit. Movements are activations of somatic thought processes. Dance is a manifestation and materialisation of embodied cognition.

As Bhutoria and Hebbani point out in their 2019 paper "Embodied Cognition: Dance, Body, and Mind,"

> Embodied cognition is the concept that our intellectual abilities such as gaining knowledge, comprehending concepts, remembering, judging, and problem solving are not confined to our brain alone. It is the idea that the body influences the mind.[2]

Their reflections are largely based on the proposals made by Varela, Thompson and Rosch in their 1992 book *The Embodied Mind*, where the notion of "enaction" was proposed, stating "that the experienced world can be portrayed and determined by mutual interactions among the physiology of the individual, its sensorimotor circuit and the environment.[3] In reference to *The Embodied Mind*, they also point out that "cognition is a dynamic sensorimotor activity and is not only conditioned by the neural activity but also essentially enacted, in that it emerges through the bodily activities of the organisms."

What Varela et al. wrote about embodied cognition in 1992[4] is something that people of African origin and probably many other Indigenous people across the globe have known for thousands of years.

It has been known to our people that our bodies have cognitive powers and can absorb impulses from our experiences around us in the physical and spiritual worlds. And since every absorber is an emitter, it is obvious that this interaction is not one-sided and thus the impulses of our bodies also shape the environments in which we find ourselves. One could understand dance as the medium through which the

35

communication between the body and the world is enabled. Dance as transmitter. As a translator?

Since that is the case, we can understand a street dance like Krump which was initiated and practiced by young African-Americans expressing strong, big, and sometimes aggressive gesticulations as an expression of what young African Americans have to experience on the streets. Krump seems to be a manifestation of anger against crimes, racial violences, class inequalities, and much more chiseled onto the body and manifested in these energy and anger-filled movements. At the same time, Krump is cathartic and transformative. And in that light, Krumpers consider the dance a kind of spiritual engagement as it allows for them to assume, accept, process, and release their emotions in that process of dancing, in a context where words are either not enough or blatantly fail them.

In this context, the music genre and dance Kpanlogo is worth looking at. Kpanlogo emerged as a youth dance and movement around the period of Ghanaian independence in 1957. The musical motifs are in the genealogy of Highlife and as well as Ga music genres like Gome, Kolomashie, and Oge. Kpanlogo is a derivative of Gbajo, which in Ga means "storytelling." Dancers of Kpanlogo are somatic narrators. The hand and leg works are very precise gesticulations of beckoning, calling, pointing sending away and other signifiers. All body parts are called into action. Sometimes dancers fit in more fabric around their buttocks to increase the size and make movements more expressive. And all in all, there is a spirit of optimism embedded in the music and dance, maybe related to the birth of a new nation? Besides the tangential narration of stories, Kpanlogo also acts as a dramatic and choreographic vessel within which stories can find form, i.e., a story narrated by mouth is translated into song and into dance movements.[5]

As a collective of thinking bodies, sometimes set in pairs, the Kpanlogo dancers thus pick up information from the outside world, process it through performativity and deliver it again. In that sense, what cognitive scientists call Enaction of Enactivism – which is to say that through the interchange or exchange between the environments and the acting organism, cognition actually emerges – is omnipresent in Kpanlogo as in many other dances.

In a documentary[6] about the Assiko/Ambas Bay, music and dance legend Salle John, he talks about some of the background of the Ambas Bay dance. In the documentary he makes the symbolic movements of the *"pia o yabassi."*[7] Both arms swing up and down, left and right mimicking the movements of rowers paddling a boat along the Nkam river in Cameroon. In this call and response music and dance, the rower-dancer gives the sign and direction and the others follow for the boat to go in the right direction. Salle John in the documentary also talks about one of his most famous songs "Bon'Essoky"[8] in which he sings about the passing of his father and all the people who came by to pay respect. He says it is a very sad song though people dance to it and then he reiterates that this is so because Ambas Bay dance is about being gay and happy. The dance becomes a space of mourning, of processing and transforming the sad occurrence of losing his father into a celebration of life, but most especially, through the music and dance all listening and dancing can collectively engage in that process of catharsis.

These aforementioned random examples go a long way to show how dance is a space of expressivity, a space of mediation between the body and its environment, and a space of affectivity, wherein different kinds of emotions are absorbed, processed and emitted.

Act IV: The Body as Text and Memory Board

In his seminal essay "What They Came with: Carnival and the Persistence of African Performance Aesthetics in the Diaspora,"[9] Esiaba Irobi poses the crucial question "Does the body have a memory?" and he goes on to answer the question by examining how Africans that were captured and translocated to the so-called new world as enslaved people, through what he calls 'kinaesthetic intelligence' carried knowledges in and through their bodies and how these knowledges inform the aesthetics and performativity of rituals and other public manifestations like carnival and other festivities everywhere where on finds African peoples across the world. These knowledges take form in ritual performances like *Candomble, Voodoo, Santeria, Lucumi, Mardi Gras, Oshun, John Konnu, Hip-Hop* and many other practices related to African peoples.

Irobi argues that,

> because the ontology of most African peoples is primarily spiritual, the physical body incorporates, at one level, habit memory through which functional activities such as climbing, sculpting, handwork, gestures, prostrations, and styles of walking are created and mastered. At the secondary modeling level (i.e., the more complex, metalingual system of communication), African societies consciously fashion a corporeal semiology through which the body becomes the symbolic repository of transcendent and expressive as well as philosophical ideas associated with religion, worship, the divine, ritual

37

ceremony, celebration, war, weddings, funerals, royalty, politics, and so on. Most of these ideas and concepts are structured and expressed through mime, music, and dance.[10]

Here I am particularly interested in how dance plays a role in the acquisition, cultivation and propagation of information. The body then becomes that repository of memories and histories, and these memories and histories can be activated whenever a dance is performed.

Bend-skin is a music and dance genre that came to prominence in Cameroon in the early 90s with the special input of the legendary musician André Marie Tala. Bend-skin came at a moment of sociopolitical transition in the country, and somehow, paradoxically, embodied some of the sociopolitical concerns and at the same time served as a distraction from many sociopolitical issues. In most of the songs, metaphors were used to express issues of labor, class questions, rural-urban complexities, as much as sexuality. In Cameroon, the popular motorbikes that plague the cities as the most effective means of transport, polluting the cities with toxic gases and noise, while at the same time serving as the magical solutions of the extremely grave traffic congestion, are called "Bend skin." The "Bend Skinneurs" are in most socio-political unrests at the forefront of agitation and manifestation. They are the bearers of a certain chaos instigation and, at the same time, chaos management. So their role in society is far more than just transporters. At the same time, Bend-skin refers to the sexual act popularly known as "doggystyle." This reference to sexuality is both to be understood literally and metaphorically as it relates to the colloquial "being screwed from behind."

During a Bend-skin dance, dancers bend over, lift up their backsides while swinging them around, and with complex foot dance movements, dance around in a circle.

So, in every Bend-skin dance, that repository of memories of sociopolitical and sociocultural issues is again put to test, readapted, replayed, re-cultivated and reincorporated again.

For the body to serve as a repository of memory, there must be a way for what is to be remembered to be written, inscribed, or encoded into it. This is done, amongst other ways, through articulated dance movements.

So if the body is a repository of memory, dance is a methodology for the recuperation of that memory.

The importance of dance in the context of the African world as a literally tool and space is aptly expressed by Esiaba Irobi when he writes:

38

On the African continent and in many parts of the African diaspora, dance, accompanied by music, represents the supreme art, the art par excellence. This is because dance, as a form of kinaesthetic literacy, is the primary medium for coding the perception of our outer and inner worlds, our transcendent worlds, our spiritual history, and the memory of that complex history. The body is the major conduit of artistic expression, whether it is a painting, a dance, a book like *The Black Atlantic*, sculpting, or performing. The medium is immaterial. The ultimate source of signification is the human body. It is therefore because the body is the primary instrument for incubating, articulating, and expressing all ideas as well as transporting all art, be it music, drama, literature, electronic messages, theater, festival, or carnival, that I want to argue that it is through phenomenology and kinaesthetic literacy (i.e., the use of the medium of the body as a site of cultural signification) that crucial aspects of Indigenous African festival theater were translocated to the New World.[11]

Irobi's kinaesthetic literacy and the understanding of the body as a site of cultural signification explain the omnipresence of bodily practices, performative phenomena, phenomenological events in many African cosmogonies, in our tales and myths, our rituals and our imaginaries of the world.

Act V: The Body and the Conjugation of Humanity

One could say that the point of intersection between Irobi's reflections on kinaesthetic literacy and Léna Blou's philosophy of *"Bigidi mè pa tonbé"* is the deep quest to understand how the body actively plays a role in not only portraying our humanity, but actually actively plays a role in its conjugation.

In her seminal essay,[12] Léna Blou discusses the concept of *"Bigidi mè pa tonbé"* in relation to the body, the Caribbean body, the African body at large, as specifically situated in dire historical and contemporary moments. The philosophy of the body as portrayed by Blou is a contemplative, a comprehensive, an adaptive, a resistant, an imaginative body, especially when it comes to *"Bigidi mè pa tonbé!"* But what exactly does *"Bigidi mè pa tonbé!"* mean? According to Léna Blou:

[...] dancing in the West Indies is a way of acting, apprehending the world, and relating to others. *"Bigidi, mè pa tonbé!"* is a popular Guadeloupean Creole expression that symbolises the vision of the world in the Caribbean perfectly. Deprived of their bodies, their time and their space [...] our ancestors drew on their brilliance by opting for a formulation of intelligence that integrated chaos as a foundation underpinning their being, as natural, preserving adaptability in the face of disorder as a lifeline, precisely by reactivating it as a redeeming weapon of resistance to preserve their humanity. During the colonial era, the 'body' as an entity was denoted as non-human, yet, in a kind of backlash, African slaves refuted this assertion.

Which is to say that the kinaesthetic literacy of the body of the enslaved people in states of maximum precarity, absorbed the chaos of the world, as much as the ounces of virtues for survival to be able to perform a life and enable the enslaved to live on. Here, the body doesn't only act as a space of resistance, but a space in which alternative ways of being are imagined, a kind of somato-imaginary, and performed.

The translation of this somato-imaginary into form can be witnessed in those Afro-descendant Caribbean dances that Blou refers to in her essay like *Kasékò* in French Guiana, *Bèlè* in Martinique and *Gwoka* in Guadeloupe, when she discusses the interplay between *Bigidi* (disorder) and the *Rèpriz* (adaptation). It goes without saying that this possibility of the body to engage with disorder and allow for adaptation is something one can find all over the African world and beyond.

In Lafabri'k, in Guadeloupe, which was founded by Léna Blou and where the second *Invocation* for the 36th Bienal de São Paulo took place, a poster was hung on which was written:

We understand that this humanity, to face disorder, responds with adaptive strategies.
We also understand that the body is the first to be impacted, by receiving the explosions of existence, of which it memorizes the memories, as well as the happy experiences, as much as the unhappy ones, which build, in this universe, a dynamic or subtle alterity.

This seems to me the crux of Blou's conjugation of humanity using the tools of *Gwoka* in general and *Bigidi* in particular. Through dance, the body becomes the medium through which humanity as a verb can be conjugated. Through dance the body becomes a space of composition, and through rehearsals and dancing, the body becomes fluent in exercising the language of humanity. Like every language, humanity too, needs to be learned. Like every language, if not practiced enough, the language skills get rusty. So too is the case with humanity, which needs to be practiced and exercized like a muscle to keep it from going numb, which seems to be our current state of the world. Like every language, the body like humanity is made up of codes that only the initiated can decode. One can be human without being initiated into the practice of humanity.

The two days of *Invocation* at Lafabri'k seemed to me a glimpse into an initiation into humanity. Especially during the *swaré-léwòz* we were fortunate to witness some of the codes of the language of humanity being displayed in the *Gwoka* dance rituals. We could witness knowledge of deep humanity being passed in that sacred space of the *swaré-léwòz*. To understand the sacrality, the social importance, the architecture and the spirit of humanity and other beings that co-exist within the space of the *swaré-léwòz*, we must go back to Léna Blou, who describes the space as such:

> The *swaré-a-léwòz* is actually an empty space that only assumes consistency in its sacralization through the human presence. The venue that hosts this popular event is an ephemeral, ecological, informal, unpredictable, and plastic non-place, in which people naturally and spontaneously arrange themselves in a circle (*lawond-a-léwòz*).

The body and dance are central in our cosmology because it is a space of literacy, a space in which cultures, histories and geographies are memorized and disseminated. The body and dance are fundamental as spaces of conceptualization of spatial strategies and social concepts. If we engage with the body and dance much deeper, we will be able to come up with alternative modes of governance and other philosophies of being together with each other in the world beyond racial, class, gender, religious, cultural and other barriers.

For if the bodies and dancing of the animals could conjure water from ancestral wells, so too can we, through performativity at large find a new spring and taste of humanity from those ancestral wells.

The tom-tom of the arena
Jump, jump, beautiful djiguène
It's the tom-tom of the arenas

who calls you tonight.
Coumba
Dazzling queen
for you
will perform the steps of
Saloum and Baol Rhythm and cadence...
And why would the moon rise
if not to illuminate
the frenetic dances?
This is only a song
The song of the tom-tom of the arenas.
Jump, jump, beautiful djiguène
It's the tom-tom of the arenas
Who calls you tonight.[13]

Excerpt from *La Ronde des jours* [The Round of Days], by Bernard Binlin Dadié.

1   Bernard Binlin Dadié, *Hommes de tous les continents*. Paris: Présence Africaine, 1967.

2   K. Bhutoria e S, Hebbani, "Embodied Cognition: Dance, Body, and Mind," *International Journal of Indian Psychology,* v.7, n.4, pp.818-824, 2019.

3   Ibid.

4   Francisco J. Varela; Evan Thompson; Eleanor Rosch, *The Embodied Mind: Cognitive Science and Human*. Cambridge: Mit Press, 1992.

5   Available at thisworldmusic.com/kpanlogo-african-drumming-dance-ghana/. Accessed on: 2025.

6   Available at www.youtube.com/watch?v=hynenke7jjA&t=88s. Accessed on: 2025.

7   Available at www.youtube.com/watch?v=dkKcKGAtOGs. Accessed on: 2025.

8   Available at www.youtube.com/watch?v=5aPsFrSw_PE. Accessed on: 2025.

9   Esiaba Irobi, "What They Came with: Carnival and the Persistence of African Performance Aesthetics in the Diaspora," *Journal of Black Studies*, v.37, n.6, pp.896-913, 2007.

10   Ibid.

11   Ibid.

12   Léna Blou, "Totter, but Never Fall! The Feint of Time, the Wandering Of The Body and the Ambigidité of the Caribbean Being" in: Olga von Schubert (ed.), *O Quilombismo: Of Resisting and Insisting, of Flight as Fight, of Other Democratic Egalitarian Political Philosophies*. Berlin: HKW, 2023.

13   Bernard Binlin Dadié, *La Ronde des jours*, Paris: Seghers, 1956.

The *Bigidi*, a Knowledge Incarnate at the Heart of the *Lawonn*

Léna Blou

I / The *Bigidi* Phenomenon

A part of the world inherits a patrimonial legacy that is danced, told, sung, and rhythmed to the sound of the vibrating drum. Caribbean people have been able to build their uniqueness over time, such as the Martinican *Bèlè*, the Guyanese *Kasékò*, or the Guadeloupean *Gwoka*. There's no denying that this is a legacy forged in the heart of colonization and enslavement in the Americas. Personally, I have always been amazed by the musical and choreographic performance of the *Gwoka* dancer inside the *Lawonn*.[1] My fascination never waned, despite my immersion in this Ka-culture, as two phenomena left me perplexed. A reality presented itself to my eyes, that of a *léwòz* dancer performing a chaotic and unstable dance, *always poised to...* And yet they never fell. *Bigidi mè pa tonbé*, revealed itself to me, and I wondered: "Why, in one place on Earth, do people dance in chaos?"

To answer this question, I looked to see if body instability existed in other dances in the Americas. My answer was irrevocable: whether in Belize, the United States, Brazil, French Guiana, Haiti, Puerto Rico, etc., I found the same pattern, that of a temporal discontinuity, contrasting gestures of movement, evasion, rupture interpreted and named differently depending on the country: *Bigidi* for the Guadeloupeans, *Nika* for the Guyanese, *Wèlto* for the Martinicans, *Kasé* for the Haitians or *Malandragem* for the Brazilians, for example.

My initial intuition, which suspected that this way of moving to the rhythm of the drums had a deeper meaning, was gradually confirmed. There is a "bigidante" inscription in Caribbean corporeality that can be read in so-called "traditional" dances: Cuban *Santeria*, Haitian *Voodoo*, Martinican *Bélè*, Puerto Rican *Bomba*, Guyanese *Kasékò*, Guadeloupean *Gwoka*, or even American *Hip-Hop*, Brazilian *Capoeira*, etc. I formulated a postulate that *Bigidi* was, in fact, a "Caribbean civilizational matrix," which defines the conception of the world from a philosophical, anthropological, sociological, political, economic, and spiritual point of view.

I then analyzed the pattern of the Guadeloupean *Bigidi*, with the aim of defining its archetype. To me, it was a question of identifying the exact moment when the *Gwoka* dance was in the *Bigidi* during its music-choreographic performance. I was able to observe three phases that implemented a form of uninterrupted fluidity through the synergistic alternation between rupture and adaptation, in which a circularity was achieved within the *Lawonn*.

45

Pòté an ganm	*Bigidi*	*Rèpriz*
Or		
Exposition	Rupture	Adaptation

Based on this scheme, I was able to identify four typologies of *bigidi* in music-choreographic performance, especially in Guadeloupe, Martinique, and French Guiana.

- → **Postural *Bigidi***: which constructs the shape or architecture of the body, privileging asymmetry.
- → **Temporal *Bigidi***: which concerns the relationship with time, focusing on its discontinuity.
- → **Ponderal *Bigidi***: between gravitation and the abstraction of body weight, where the "bigidante" body game is established between the high and low levels.
- → **Cultural *Bigidi***: transgression of the formalized musical-choreographic universe through a system of bricolage and inversion.

I was convinced that bodily chaos had an ontological meaning, from which comes the need, in my view, to identify the factors that contributed to generating such a unique way of moving. In my research, I opted for a sensitive approach so as not to erase the human dimension of the phenomenon of enslavement. I refused to accept a de-spiritualized and unaffected view of enslavement. It must be remembered that an enslaved person is first and foremost a human being. I have identified two founding factors that sowed the seeds of *Bigidi* in the bodies and minds: history and nature. The first factor, history, is built around four key moments: uprooting, de-identification, dehumanization, and racialization. And de-spatialization is combined with the second factor: nature.

First Factor: History

First *Bigidi:* Uprooting

I believe that being uprooted from African soil is the first quasi-matricial *Bigidi.* The individual undergoes a radical spatial change, from being a free human being standing on their land to being horizontal in a closed, dark space. Without knowing why, they find themselves lying down in the midst of an incessant rocking inside the enslaver ship, unable to move to the right or to the left, in a state of expectation and uncertainty.

It's a physical and kinaesthetic *Bigidi*, in that the feel both horizontally stable and paradoxically unstable due to the movement of the sea. But this *Bigidi* is also emotional and psychological, because the being is invaded by despair, fear, and anxiety. It is destabilized. The nature and perception of the experience are understood as the difference between the experience of a free person inscribed in a social coherence and the experience of being held captive by a plundering organization. Being uprooted from the land is the key moment that brings into play the immediacy of two founding and synergistic principles: chaos equals adaptation, or *Bigidi* equals *Rèpriz*.[2] The hold of the slave ship is, in a sense, the symbolic abyss of a new humanity in the making. *Bigidi* is consubstantial with *Rèpriz*; it is deposited in the heart of humanity, where its foundations are progressively developed and transmitted from generation to generation as a structuring and inevitable social fact.

Second *Bigidi*: De-identification

The second *Bigidi* is the irreversible loss of the individual's identity and lineage. They will never hear their name again. The being suffers from a disorientation of parentage and identity. A form of generality surrounds his Blackness, *pièce d'Inde*[3]... Then, once they arrive at their new home, their master will usually give them a nickname, as they would for an object or an animal, for example: Fatty, No Worries, Rabbit, Pigeon, Honey Loaf, etc. The individual, confronted with the *imbalance* of identity, responds with a mental and intellectual adaptation, the command of silence. Silence, an adaptive solution to best regulate the complexity of inhabiting this fluctuating and versatile identity. The process of this principle is not to name the real. The individual can even reconstruct a device for reaffiliation from vague and random references that have nothing to do with marital status. For example, my mother, depending on places or people: Blou/institution, Gueret/friends, Doudou/family, Hélène/recent relationship, Bichara/sister. This is an adaptive re-identification based on a poly-identitarian culture. We need to think of silence as a general taxonomy that will designate singular but polysemic things, since several things or people can be designated by a common term that ultimately has a meaning or designates different and unrelated realities.

Third *Bigidi*: Dehumanization

"We declare that 'slaves' are movable property," says article 44 of the royal edict of March 1685 of the Black Code, classifying and relegating enslaved people to the category of objects. This third *Bigidi* reaches an absolute degree of intensity. The enslaved being ceases to be human in the eyes of the white man. He is banished from the circle of humanity. It is the entity "body" that is designated as non-human. In response, the enslaved person will magnify this by putting all his knowledge into it through culture (dance, music, storytelling, singing...). The intellectuality of the being will be revealed, as well as understanding, invention, creativity, sensitivity, aesthetics, the vision of the world through the body. It is precisely through the *Bigidi mask* that the body becomes an instrument of protest to preserve its humanity.

Fourth *Bigidi*: Racialization

"The image of the African, of the Black man, does not originate in Africa, but in the Caribbean."[4] The need for hegemony and domination led Europeans to invent race. Skin color would become the central "natural" attribute that would distinguish men from each other, from the whitest to the Blackest, thus implying their social hierarchy. This fourth *Bigidi* adds to the previous ones, where the individual needs to understand that the color of their skin conditions them in a new social relationship of dominant-dominated. Their *Rèpriz* in this new social framework is marginalization. They will create their *Karékò*. This *Karékò* represents both the space and the symbolic time of the body. It's important to remember that at the time of enslavement, the settler was the master of the enslaved's body, space, and time. The latter had to operate a dual relationship with the body, one for the master and the other for themselves. In the context of housing, they offer their *kadav* [corpse], i.e. only their mechanical strength. Once a person is dead, they no longer hear, see, or feel, they are only a *kadav*. The enslaved person and their descendants will transcend this limited body, having the ability to withdraw from their body, leaving only the *kadav* whose role is to perform work or some other function from which they derive no benefit or pleasure. The being can symbolically re-incorporate their inner *kò* [body] and thus have direct access to their inner being, which is revealed only to themselves and those like them. It is the *kò* that the individual can summon and inhabit at will, even if only in spiritual form. This body, the [*kò*], is the property of the individual and is manifested in their spaces of freedom, which are their *kaz* [house], their *jadèn kréyol* [Creole courtyard], and their own body. We must understand that it is precisely the articulation of these three symbolic spaces that constitutes and represents the concept of *Karékò*. And it is precisely at this moment that the enslaved human becomes a person! It is the

48

habitat of the being, a body-space where the being is free to circulate through its imaginaries, where it expresses itself, speaks, thinks, moves, and dances within this metaphysical body. It can be accessed very precisely, especially in the context of the *Lawonn* of the *Gwoka*, the *véyé boukoussou* [funeral rites], carnival, or informal family celebrations. In this way, and in these marginal spaces, the individual will initiate procedures, devices, organizations, and management to reintegrate amputated social functions (economic, educational, health, spiritual, etc.), such as Maroon societies like the *Bushinengé* in Guyana, the Mutual Aid Societies in Martinique, the *swaré-léwòz* in Guadeloupe, *Candomblé* in Brazil, *Voodoo* in Haiti, etc.

Second Factor: Nature

Fifth *Bigidi*: De-spatialization

Once dispersed in the various colonies (Brazil, Barbados, Haiti, Guadeloupe, Cuba...), the enslaved people had to adapt to a new space *hic* e *nunc* [here and now]. This space is undoubtedly reconfigured for the colonial project, but it also highlights the second factor that feeds *Bigidi*. American nature is chaotic and makes people dance because of its unpredictability: hurricanes, earthquakes, tsunamis, volcanic eruptions, and the opacity of the Amazon rainforest. Thus, the African human deported to America invents the mechanism of bricolage, inversion, simulation, *masko* (camouflage), fluctuation, plasticity, and mental agility to respond efficiently to the multiple *Bigidi* of his existence.

II / The Concept of Lawonn

It is at the heart of the *Lawonn* that the *Bigidi* expresses itself most intensely, like "a breath of the world."[5]

The *Lawonn* thus plays a protective, federative, and socializing role, as it is a place that fosters empathy, individual freedom, democracy, inclusion, acceptance of self and others, mutual aid, solidarity, and *fap-fap* creation/improvisation. It is *Lawonn*'s secure sociality that allows *Bigidi* to blossom into a necessary *circularity*, i.e. the plastic and improbable circulation from one space to another (dance, singing, drumming, *bik* [restoration], *lasistans* [audience]. Gilbert Laumord, a PhD candidate in Theater Arts, calls this phenomenon intra-*Lawonn*. In fact, all the

49

individualities that make up the *Lawonn* are in interaction, in synergy, and connected thanks to the phenomenon of *Rèpriz*. The *Lawonn* is a wonderful example of social cohesion and coexistence, whose cornerstone of harmony in *disorder* is built around *fap-fap* and *Rèpriz*. "*Bigidi* thus presents a model of understanding the world that considers the body as a node of knowledge."[6]

Conclusion

The heirs of this history (Afro-descendants) are constantly confronted with *imbalances*. It's a form of entropy that never stops and which is present at all latitudes of their lives (physical, psychological, spatial, economic, and personal primal shocks). The philosophy of *Bigidi mè pa tonbé* is a mental posture that has been silently handed down to us by our ancestors, built around bricolage, detour, feinting, dodging, camouflage, silence, *fap-fap*, temporal discontinuity, the art of complexity, and inhabited silence, etc., even adaptability – even when illogical – in order to simply honor life. Hélène Migerel, a psychologist from Guadeloupe, believes that "refusing to fall," avoiding the fall in the *Bigidi* process, preserves the individual's self-esteem and psychological integrity.[7]

I'll end by quoting French choreographer Bernard Montet on his understanding of *Bigidi*:

> *Bigidi* would be our universal. A dance of Relation that concerns each and every one of us, regardless of our age, culture, or history. That each of us can re-appropriate to make it our own matrix, our own foundation [...] Imbalance as a space of freedom, of regaining control of who we are as individuals and members of a community, that of human beings. Imbalance as the center of human consciousness. A catharsis that keeps the spiritual eye open to the truth.[8]

1   *Lawonn* is Creole and means *la-ronde* "as in the tradition of West Indian evenings. The old la-ronde consisted of an assembly around a guy who was going to express a breath of existence: dancing or giving voice. [...] A *la-ronde* was a creative space. [...] We couldn't find a better place in the world to share what we carry within ourselves, so..." See Patrick Chamoiseau, *Le Conteur, la nuit et le panier*. Paris: Editions du Seuil, 2021, p.5.

2   A regulation melorhythm that is specified and formulated according to each *Gwoka* rhythm (it is the dancer who requests it during their performance). It is also a keyword that means harmonizing with oneself and the environment. It is a concept that regulates chaos by means of a perpetual and renewed adaptation, both physical, psychic, and spiritual, to the extent of the *disorder*.

3   Gabriel Entiope, *Nègres, danse et résistance: La Caraïbe du XVIIe au XIXe siècle*. Paris: L'Harmattan,1996, p.50. The term *"pièce d'Inde"* came to be used as a reference book value for the sales of people that took place in Black Africa as part of the Atlantic enslaved trade.

4   Ibid., p.15.

5   Hadley Galbraith, *Bigidi Memory of Survival: Embodying the Inheritance of Resilience under Slavery in Text, Film, and Performance.* Iowa: The University of Iowa, 2022.

6   Ibid.

7   Hélène Migerel, "Maladie, culture, croyances: quelles alliances" *3ème Congrès International de Soins Palliatifs*: *"Partager par-delà les frontières,"* 2016, helenmigerel.com/maladie-culture-croyances-alliances/. Accessed on: 2025.

8   Annex n. 19, text by choreographer Bernard Montet dated from 2018, in Léna Blou, Le *Bigidi,* la danse de l'harmonie du désordre: Immanence sociale du corps dansant des Antilles et de la Guyane. Guadeloupe: Université des Antilles, 2021.

To Totter Is Not to Fall: *Bigidi* in Five Replies

Keyna Eleison

Reflections on the act of stumbling... To stumble (or to totter), you have to know the ground, know what's below and what's above, be aware of the law of gravity and not understand it as a law. Stumbling is a gesture that challenges not physics but our rigid interpretation of it. It means recognizing that the ground is not just a support surface, but a space for dialogue, a presence that responds to the body's touch with an energy that is both welcoming and propulsive.

Tumbling requires intimacy with the ground, with its textures, its resistance and acceptance. You have to feel the weight of your own body, but also the lightness that comes from allowing yourself to fall without fear, transforming the impact into an encounter, the imbalance into choreography. What is "below" and what is "above" cease to be fixed opposites and become transitory states in constant negotiation.

Gravity is a dance partner. It guides but does not define. Stumbling is an act of deep listening to the body and space, a conscious choice to flirt with risk in order to discover new ways of being and moving. It's accepting vulnerability not as weakness but as creative power, as the possibility of being reborn in the moment of falling, of reinventing oneself in the brief silence between falling and getting up.

Stumbling is not about defying gravity, but about doubting it as a restriction, about bringing doubt as a proposal, as a cry, as a rhythm. It is a call to disobey the logic of weight, of control that pulls downwards, and instead to experience stumbling as a creative gesture, imbalance as a choice. A verb that refuses to accept the possibility of falling, or to see it as failure, finality, or completion, and transforms it into an opening, into the possibility of a different reading of the body in space. It's not about overcoming gravity, but negotiating with it, like dancing with a partner who leads and is led at the same time. Stumbling is also a gesture of listening, a way of feeling the world with your skin on the ground, of recognizing that the body is made up of encounters between what yields and what resists, between what is released and what is held.

The ground is no longer below, but a partnership with what is understood to be above. The ground is no longer a limit but an accomplice. You can touch the ground and feel its caress in return, the spiral impulse that doesn't push you away, but welcomes you and responds. The ground is skin, a sensitive membrane that registers contact and returns it in the form of an impulse, a resonance. Touching the ground is a conversation, a dialog between weight and lightness, between falling and rising, between collapse and reinvention. The floor is not there to hold us down; it's there to remind us that to touch is also to be touched. It is a surface of memory, where every mark, every pressure, every vestige tells a story of

53

bodies that have passed, fallen, and risen. The ground is a silent witness to the persistence of movement, of the gesture repeated and transformed.

Stumbling and touching the ground are therefore acts of radical trust. Trust that the body knows how to fall and how to get up, that the movement doesn't end on impact, but continues in spirals, in subterranean breathing. The ground is an inverted mirror, reflecting not what we see, but what we feel when we surrender to the weight and, paradoxically, find lightness in this gesture. Each fall is a rehearsal of infinity, a choreography of doubt that never closes, but expands in possibilities. And in this cycle of falling and pushing, the body learns to fly without leaving the ground.

Neither above nor below, neither right nor wrong, neither dead nor alive. Existing and affirming existence, without words — which can be limiting — but with movements, sounds and perceptions. Stumbling as a curve, and together, collectively, in knowledge, in formation.

Divestiture: Dressing up as Place, Ideas, and Presence

In Guadeloupe, I experienced the adventure of being naked.

Not the nakedness of the body, but the nakedness of the ego, of the weight of the ideas I had brought with me, of the layers of certainties. Each garment I left behind was a farewell, a gesture of abandonment of my own prejudices.

There, among rhythms that speak more than words, I discovered that to be clothed is not an act of passivity, but of active surrender.

The place covered me with the smell of the sea, the ideas adorned me with the threads of what is collective, and the people, with their generous gaze, embroidered new layers of understanding about who I could be.

I was stripped, not as someone who loses, but as someone who gains space for something greater. And in that empty space, I was filled with gestures that only being there could teach me:

a dance that is in no rush;
a conversation that moves to the rhythm of the waves;
an intimacy made up of smiles and silences.

Allowing yourself to be dressed is accepting the unknown. It's allowing the ground you walk on to shape your step, the music you hear to compose your breath. It wasn't fabrics that covered me, but stories:

54

a weave of resistance and celebration;
a seam of intertwined pasts;
a fabric that insists on being future.

By undressing, I saw that the clothes we wear — real or
symbolic — often limit us. And by letting the place dress us, we become
part of it. We stop being visitors and become accomplices in its existence.
In the end, I didn't go back to dressing like I used to. I carry what
Guadeloupe gave me:

An invisible garment made of shared humanity, in which each
thread is a memory that reminds me;
that being naked is sometimes the shortest way to being whole.

Stumbling is not falling. Falling is giving in to the weight, it's the
unexpected collapse, the moment when control breaks down. Stumbling, on
the other hand, is an extremely conscious gesture, or at least an invitation
to intense awareness. It's a movement that carries intention, even in its
apparent disorder. Stumbling is making room for imbalance without fearing
it, it's listening to the body as it tilts beyond the safe axis. It's not loss, but
transition; it's not the end, but the pause between one state and another.
Stumbling is recognizing that the ground is part of the journey.
The body that falls learns its boundaries and its expansions. While falling
can be seen as failure, this is binary, has a limit and a limiting dimension;
stumbling is an act of transformation, a curve in the path. It is the body that
accepts vulnerability not as weakness, but as power, as the possibility of
reconfiguring itself in the encounter with the ground and, from there, reinventing the impulse to continue.

Gravity, this force that insists on anchoring us to the ground, is more than a
physical principle; it is a metaphor for power structures that want to keep us
in fixed, delimited places, safe for those in control. It carries the weight of
the norm, of knowledge that wants to be universal, of stability that echoes
the echo of Eurocentric voices, always trying to define what is high and
what is low, what is center and what is margin.
But to stumble... ah, to stumble is to laugh in the face of it all. It is
laughing out loud, with your whole body, because laughter is also a fall — an
explosion that destabilizes, that dismantles the theater from the seriousness
of its structures. Stumbling is a knowledge of the body that understands
that balance is a comfortable illusion for those who fear movement. Stumbling is ancestral, it is insubordinate, it is intelligence

that is written in the gesture that deliberately fails, that stumbles to find
other paths on the ground. The body that topples dances with gravity, but
does not obey it. It negotiates, questions, provokes.

Stumbling is a gesture of radical disobedience. A body that
refuses to stand, simply because it has been told that the "right" thing to do
is to remain upright. Stumbling is the politics of affection with the ground,
with imbalance, with creative failure. It is the art of falling, knowing that
the ground is not an end, but a continuation, a fertile territory for reinvention. Every stumble is a trace of resistance, a choreography of possible
worlds that don't fit into the straight lines of colonial thinking.

When one chooses to stumble, the body challenges the myth of
perpetual ascent, of linear productivity. It shatters the illusion of centrality,
of power that wants to be vertical. The stumble is a cry for freedom that
reverberates, a gesture of insubmission that transforms collapse into
creative power. The ground gives us back not only the impact, but the echo
of all the bodies that have fallen before, that have laughed, that have
resisted, that have invented other ways of existing. Stumbling is a laughter
that dances in the face of gravity, an indomitable response to the arrogance
of structures that think they can define us.

I will not recognize the fall!
It just won't come.

Debt to Dance, Debt to Speak in the Caribbean Space

Olivier Marboeuf

Vigils and Circles

In 2018, with the closure of Espace Khiasma, the non profit art center in the northeastern suburbs of Paris that I founded and ran for fifteen years, I found myself without a venue and an orphan of a community. A community where art workers, activists, and families from the neighborhood met, those close and those distant. Although I had always thought that the spirit of the place was more important than the physical place itself, its infrastructure, and its team, this closure was a real challenge for me. It forced me to return to an essential question about place: what are we attached to and what do we support? In other words, what keeps us on our feet – allows us to stand up – and which, in turn, we *maintain*.[1] While I decided to move away from art institutions for a while, to not do elsewhere what I had been doing for all these years in this very special place, I didn't give up on this idea of instituting, of *creating a place*. On the contrary, I was returning to the essence of this gesture that had guided my work until then: to animate a community and its space of critical hospitality. A place that wasn't initially thought of as an affinity, although we had to constantly learn to take collective responsibility for its necessary maintenance and its future.

My literary and research residency at the Ateliers Médicis in 2019, in Clichy-sous-Bois, in the Paris suburbs, began at this moment of my own particular questioning, while, at the same time, the gentrification of the capital's lower-class suburbs began to take a turn as massive as it was tragic. I felt that a page of the suburb where I grew up was being violently turned. A sense of urgency to preserve stories that would soon disappear under the bulldozers. As had happened in Athens, Rio, or London, the horizon of the Olympic Games was that of the radical conclusion of a colonization of territories that were once despised. It is *terraformation*[2] itself, where territorial gentrification was accompanied by a cultural gentrification of the legacies and ways of life of minorities. Everything seemed set to produce a delicious politics of recognition and visibility, which one cannot ignore as now signaling the new regimes of land predation. Symbolic transactions are nothing more than smokescreens for what is at stake at the material level.[3] The great art institutions and cultural industries were therefore embarking on this same sequence and with great fanfare on an ephemeral and superficial "decolonial turn."[4] In France, this "turn" would take the form of an illusory policy of inclusion and diversity that did little to mask the war being waged simultaneously against the poor, migrant workers, "Islamo-leftist" intellectuals, political feminists, Muslims, militant associations and that vast suburban population that had become a nuisance. This cultural gentrification suddenly fell in love with Black and Arabic flowing rituals, only spoke of prodigious grandmothers and their healing plants, and lived under the roof of native dreams, while on the other hand not caring about a profound and needed change in the infrastructure destroying the living conditions in all these desirable worlds. This hysterical acceleration of cultural commodification has, it is true, offered unexpected opportunities to a whole generation of artists and minority cultural workers in the Global North. But no real prospects. We are now going through this *zombie moment* where the discourse of diversity of the great art institutions accompanies and accommodates itself to the destruction of diversity, the progressive disappearance of the multiplicity of associative spaces that made up the rich critical and creative fabric of the great European capitals. As with the climate crisis, it seems naive and, at the very least, dangerous to underestimate the irreversible destruction of some of our material living conditions by invoking the idea of resilience. The Earth can only repair itself under certain conditions. The same applies to the existences that make it up. They will only rise from the fall if they have maintained, cultivated something deep enough, a foundation from which it will be possible to re-establish places for dignified lives. It is true that, even in the worst hours of the plantation, the fungibility of enslaved human beings never reached its full realization; the captives never stopped refusing to become *matter to be exhausted*. But the real condition for them to *recover* their humanity (the "reprise" of humanity), based on that *deep and hidden humanity* of the enslaved, was marronage. Not only for those who escaped, but also for those who still lived on the plantation. Because by creating a radical exteriority, marronage undid the narrative supremacy of this place of non-being and dehumanization. It pointed to another place, another possible basis for "reprise" (retaking) and sustained the daily practice of psychic extraction of the *enslaved in himself* in order to practice *becoming human* in a different way.

As I begin my 2019 literary residency in Clichy-sous-Bois in this twilight atmosphere of a moldy festival of diversity, I wonder about the existence of this base, which I then call "an invisible popular,"[5] in the sense of a form of minority cultural life, capable of resisting "commoditization." In a sense, a resistant way of *creating a place* to remain, to catch one's breath. Clichy-sous-Bois has been a symbolic town in the suburbs of Paris since two young men, Zyed Benna and Bouna Traoré, were electrocuted to death in 2005 – and a third seriously injured – while trying to flee the police. At the time, these deaths sparked a vast movement of revolt in working-class neighborhoods throughout the French suburbs. A feeling of belonging to something that is both morbid – lives that are worth less than others – and powerful – lives capable of defying the necropolitics of the

60

French state through fire and refusing to disappear in silence. Lives that escaped the news, the shadows of a national history of which they were not a part. This tragic event and the revolts that followed marked an era and the particular formulation of the French decolonial movement that followed. As happened later with the Adama Committee (created after the death of Adama Traoré in a police station in the north suburbs of Paris in 2016), a form of *Black monumentality* was built around the death of the young men of Clichy-sous-Bois. In other words, a way of keeping the dead among the living. This affirmation of a refusal of an unworthy death and the contemptuous lie of the police, this radical desire to produce the conditions for justice (and no longer just demand it) constitute this particular monumentality that takes the form of marches, festivals, and soccer tournaments every year. By returning to Clichy-sous-bois, I was committing myself to participating in this fluid and living monument in a period of urban transition where I was also beginning to ask myself how to tell the discreet story of the Caribbean diasporas in Paris.[6] This moment of confusion and discouragement led me to become interested in the form of the vigil. The vigil as a practice of mourning, but also as a space for the circulation of speech and story in traditional West Indian *lakou*. This interest would later expand to other practices of the circle; the Afro-Brazilian capoeira *roda*, which would become a second family for my eldest son, or the Guadeloupean *léwoz circle* (*Lawonn*), spaces where a community *held together* because you don't always get up from a fall and, more importantly, you never get up alone.

Something sustains us and we have to learn to maintain it, to maintain this particular nature of a culture without spectacle or externality. In *léwoz*, no one can be left out of the *circle*. Because it's not just a show of music and singing, it is a place of collective memory that is erected and updated from the infrastructure of bodies and musical instruments, from the almost nothingness of misery, from the breath of life. However, being at a distance is the very condition of cultural extraction that requires being outside the contingencies and responsibilities of the *circle*. Outside its history. And this is where this practice of commoditization and cultural extraction exhausts the objects it focuses on. It was on this path that I came across a certain enthusiasm for choreographer Léna Blou's research and practice around *Bigidi*.[7] She evoked, in a very fair way, this way of maintaining yourself in this almost nothingness that you couldn't imitate without implicating yourself in the ecology of the *circle*, that you couldn't borrow without giving a part of yourself in return. In fact, you can't fake the collapse, because the collapse of the West Indies is also that of the

 body bending under the weight of a debt that few people want to share. They can take everything from you, but the debt will always remain. Just as this movement towards the ground is peculiar, the way we rise from this encounter with death is unique because it relies on the invisible forces of a place, present and past, real and virtual. More than a dance, *Bigidi* is an archive, an archive of material and psychological conditions. That's why Léna's work was important for my own research into the Caribbean archive and how this corporeal and fragile archive resisted fungibility and transmitted itself by being reinterpreted. It's a theme that has taken on a significant place in my work in recent years and which has fed into the many conversations I've been able to have with artists, researchers and activists, such as the Guadeloupean artist Eddy Firmin, or the Haitian academic and author Stéphane Martelly.[8]

Installments and Interruptions

If we look at the archive from the perspective of the collective maintenance of a place that needs to be constantly rebuilt, the term "reprise" takes on a double meaning. It is, first and foremost, the gesture of collectively rising from a difficulty – the *Rèpriz* after the *Bigidi* – because those who recompose themselves raise the entire place of speech and dance as a whole through a reciprocal commitment, an alliance of forces. But "reprise" can also be a way of naming the effort to maintain the continuity of a shared history through successive repetitions, which turn the archive into a form that is always to come, but filled with its past utterances, an echo chamber. This technique of affected repetition[9] (a repetition that crosses a body that affects it and transforms it in return) makes up a place of memory and reparation that undoes the illusory discontinuities produced by multiple interruptions and dispersions. In my essay "Suites décoloniales: sortir de la plantation" [Decolonial Sequences: Exiting the Plantation], I deal at length with a rereading of Sylvia Wynter's "Novel and History, Plot and Plantation."[10] In this emblematic text, the Jamaican author turns the literary genre of the novel into a fragment, a *plot* whose multiplication points to the existence of another narrative regime, distinct from the great plantation novel. A narrative regime that Wynter refuses to leave in the state of incidents, of short episodes of revolt and rupture that would briefly disturb the surface and the continuous plot of the established order. On the contrary, it urges us to make the effort to connect the pieces in order to give body to the continuum of another minority history that is itself interrupted by the narrative forces of the plantation. What this text mainly tells us is that the refusal of fungibility, the revolt in the face of injustice, the desire for humanity and freedom are constants in the Caribbean history of emancipation and not exceptions. In the same way that the Haitian revolution cannot be

62

considered a mere incident in the great history of French democracy, a lost and isolated struggle, but must be restored as the plot of one of the most radical and influential projects of emancipation in colonial modernity.[11]

It is in this specific light that cultural appropriation needs to be studied again. Not just limiting it to an act of predation by the cognitive capitalist, but also taking an interest in cultural appropriation as a logic of interruption of a continuum. In short, not only for what it steals and capitalizes on, but also for what it prevents. Because cultural appropriation requires, first of all, an extraction (staying outside the contingencies of the *circle*) and a commoditization (transforming the *circle* itself into an autonomous and "transplantable" cultural artifact). This double movement of extraction/commodification is radically opposed to the relational ecology of the *léwoz* (like that of the vigil or the circle) and its specific dynamic of peer-to-peer transmission of incorporated archives. The question then arises of how to develop contemporary artistic practices that are not the result of interruptions/extractions, but which, on the contrary, contribute to producing and enriching the conditions of continuity, existence, and invention of sovereign and autonomous practices. Reflecting on this relational ecology seems to me to be a more productive way of imagining an ethic (and therefore an aesthetic) of Caribbean creation that does not exempt artists from this region and its diasporas from questioning their own ways of producing. This situation needs to be approached materialistically and not just from the point of view of identities, since we have seen that the appropriation of land and the destruction of living conditions can very well be accompanied by transactions in the symbolic economy.[12] It is worth saying that recognition and visibility are most often not offered to those who are dispossessed and expelled, but to other social classes that supposedly represent them.

63

The commodification of the Caribbean goes hand in hand with its meta-phorization, which is another way of extracting the region from its situated materiality, and especially of forgetting how a large part of the population lives. That is why it seemed essential to me to contribute to a situated Caribbean poetics, linked to the experiences of a specific body, a body-landscape that restores human perception within a connected world, human and non-human. To return to the body as an instrument of a sovereign and barrier-free place, but not to the flesh as fungible and available matter. Nor to a project of identity that would place human desire at the top of the forest in a solitary singularity. To defend a materialist poetics is to affirm at the same time a poetics of matter, of biological, physical, and thermodynamic processes, but also a poetics of material conditions, capable of perceiving in excluded bodies, in bodies in excess, in bodies in struggle and in the creativity of the roughest Caribbean lifestyles, the expression of an *archive in Bigidi*. It is this experience of a speaking body, permeated by stories and flows, that is at the origin of "Debt to Speak," a text that I presented for the first time at Léna Blou's Fabri'K in Pointe-à-Pitre in December 2024, accompanied by the musicians Guy Fromager and Aldo Midleton, during an *Invocation* of the Bienal de São Paulo.[13] I then entrusted this same text to the artist and storyteller Catherine Dénécy (known as Ca.Dé), who allowed herself to be inhabited by this figure of a woman on the verge of collapse, stumbling around in the twilight of the Guadeloupean villages. This familiar figure of the *madwoman* is to me the site of a valuable archive. She is an echo of another figure, the despeaker, the one who creolizes the French language in Édouard Glissant, the one who spills his verbal delirium to the point of exhaustion in the great Haitian poet Frankétienne. The debt to dance of Léna Blou's *Bigidi* becomes here a debt to speak, a movement of "reprise" of those who have been dispossessed, who have nothing left to lose and are stirring up secret knowledge on the edge of the precipice of their lives.

> I have a debt to speak of
> that kind of thing
> you know
> it's a cascade of mud
> in my stomach
> a cascade of voices
> inside me
> the glistening and sweet

torso
of nèg-gwo-siwo images
I have diabetes
from these images
I piss
day and night
I swear to you
a veritable torrent of bad thoughts
of bad words
I can't stop
the voices of others
that run through me
who can stop it?
Who can
hold the water
in their hands?
Who can
Repair leaks
in the
huge and rusty net
on the island
Who can?

Through this body, Caribbean fluidity, the supposed liquidity of the region's cultures, takes on a different direction, a different tone. Water is no longer just the material of journeys and the metaphor for the changing identities of creolization, it is also the secretion of sick bodies[14] and the undrinkable fluid that too often flows from the faucets of Guadeloupean homes.[15] The womb is also alternately the site of the violence of women's reproductive labor and the place of digestion/transmission of histories and revolutions.[16] *A womb-archive* that these women without compass also share with birds in a strange interspecific alliance. As all beings and things in this West Indian world participate in a *Bigidi*, the Creole houses collapse too, and the birds are not just light, cross-border messengers; they also willingly let themselves fall like the Great Gosiers that burst endlessly onto the surface of the sea and mimic this inimitable way of dying while remaining alive.

but people
really
don't want to hear
the torrent
that runs through me
they say:
what does that crazy woman mean?
and of whom I try to tell you
with my words
because they don't want to
listen to the voices
that are raving
and drifting in all this water
it's too much water
for their small brains
And that's why
the water is brown
in the faucet of my speech

Sound Tapestry, Recomposition, and Despeaking Mixture

The "Debt to Speak" text is intended for a sound creation, *Péyi en retour*, which combines poetic readings, fragments of interviews and archives, sound materials, and songs recorded with Guadeloupean musicians and Haitian artists. I started this sound work in parallel with my research on the vigil in 2019, with the idea of recomposing precarious communities around a conversation *circle*. With the Covid crisis, these communities would become spaces of solidarity, bringing together different geographies at a distance. It was a way of re-establishing a common ground between the *péyis* of the Caribbean and their diasporas, but also with those who, as in Haiti, could no longer leave their island.[17] These sound pieces make up a speculative archive, readily cacophonous, taking up the strategy of opacity in Creole conversation, where listening takes place in the midst of interference and saturation from the shards of intertwined voices.[18] These sound pieces are themselves produced in a game of "reprise" and it is not uncommon to find a fragment of one in the next, like the infinite expansion of an archive.

Progressively, along with these sound creations, I began to develop graphic works: large murals drawn *in situ* with chalk on walls painted ultramarine blue, where fragments of stories cohabit like the visual weaving of multiple plots. These graphic and improvised scores leave room for multiple interpretations and many potential stories. These *blueprints* make up a form of precarious, impermanent cinema, through the uncertain and mutable dialog they establish between sounds and images. Anyone who enters this home where the present and the absent, the living and the dead, a community in the making come together, commits themselves to an exercise in viewing potential, fugitive, delirious films: *a despeaking cinema.*[19]

1 The expression *"entre-tenir"* evokes a community that supports each other through reparation, but also through conversation (*"entretien"*), as a "holding (*tenir*) between one another (*entre*)" that continues in our care (*"entretien"*) for her. Collective speech is understood here as care that does not incur debt. See Olivier Marboeuf, "Entre-tenir, A Living Archive of Emancipation (published as part of my Banister Fletcher Global Fellowship 2023/2024, organized by the University of London Institute in Paris). Available at www.london.ac.uk/institute-paris/research/distant-islands-spectral-cities/entre-tenir-living-archive-emancipation. Accessed on: 2025.

2 See, for example, on urban terraformation, Joy White, *Terraformed: Young Black Lives in the Inner City.* London: Repeater Books, 2020.

3 Eve Tuck and K. Wayne Yang, "Decolonization is not a metaphor," *Decolonization, Indigeneity, Education & Society*, v.1, n.1, 2012.

4 Olivier Marboeuf, *Suites décoloniales: s'enfuir de la plantation.* Rennes: Editions du Commun, 2022.

5 See Olivier Marboeuf, "An Invisible Common," 2020. Available at olivier-marboeuf.com/2020/05/13/un-populaire-invisible/. Accessed on: 2025.

6 See my project "Distant Islands, Spectral Cities" Available at www.london.ac.uk/institute-paris/research/distant-islands-spectral-cities. Accessed on: 2025.

7 Olivier Marboeuf, 2022, op. cit., *Suites Décoloniales: sortir de la plantation,* pp.122-125, "Veillées et politique de la fréquence."

8 Olivier Marboeuf, "L'Archive comme lieu spéculatif," in: Conférence et Conversation avec Stéphane Martelly. *Toujours Debout*, 2023. Stéphane Martelly. Available at: olivier-marboeuf.com/2023/04/02/larchive-comme-lieu-speculatif-conference-et-conversation-avec-stephane-martelly-fr/. Accessed on: 2025.

9 In French, *"répétition"* means "repetition" or "rehearsal."

10 Sylvia Wynter, "Novel and History, Plot and Plantation," *Savacou*, n.5, pp.95-102, 1971.

11 Pierre-Franklin Tavarès, "Hegel et Haïti ou le silence de Hegel sur Saint-Dominique," *Chemins Critiques*, v.2, n.3, 1992; Susan Buck-Morse, *Hegel, Haiti and the Universal History.* Pittsburgh: University of Pittsburgh Press, 2009.

12 See Glen Sean Coulthard, *Red Skin, White Masks: Rejecting the Colonial Politics of Recognition.* Minneapolis: University of Minnesota Press, 2014.

13 The title of this lecture-performance was "Dans le ventre des oiseaux, dans la bouche des femmes sauvages" [In the Belly of Birds, in the Mouths of Wild Women].

14 Guadeloupe and Martinique have one of the highest incidences of prostate cancer in the world. This phenomenon has long been presented as a credible link to the population's African origins.

However, research by Inserm [Institut National de la Santé et de la Recherche Médicale] on pesticides and health, published in 2021, concluded that there is a strong presumption of a link between the exposure to chlordecone (a pesticide used in banana cultivation of this region) of the general population and the risk of prostate cancer (Agence Nationale de Sécurité Sanitaire de l'Alimentation, "Chlordécone aux Antilles: les risques liés à l'exposition alimentaire," 2024. Available at www.anses.fr/fr/content/chlordecone-aux-antilles-les-risques-lies-a-lexposition-alimentaire. Accessed on: 2025.

15   See "La crise de l'eau en Guadeloupe transforme le quotidien en enfer," avaiable at reporterre.net/En-Guadeloupe-la-crise-de-l-eau-s-intensifie-et-l-Etat-reduit-les-credits. Accessed on: 2025.

16   See, for example, Françoise Vergès, *The Wombs of Women: Race, Capital, Feminism.* Durham and New York: Duke University Press, 2020.

17   *The Wake/Les Veillées: A Tapestry of Voices and Thoughts, Sound and Live Music*, an online event hosted by Savvy Contemporary (Berlin), I co-curated in 2021. Accessed on: 2025.

18   See the Museum of Breath project, five soundworks for the Berlin Biennale in 2022. Available at 12.berlinbiennale.de/artists/olivier-marboeuf/.

19   Olivier Marboeuf, "Towards a Despeaking Cinema (A Caribbean Hypothesis)," *The Living Journal*, an online magazine commissioned by the Open City Documentary Festival, co-edited with Ana Vaz. Available at opencitylondon.com/. Accessed on: 2025.

Chaos vs. Order: On Being in Control by Tottering in Chaos

Anna Roberta Goetz

When I observe a *Gwoka* dancer, I [associate their movement] with drunkenness, a body that is not under control, is non-conceptualized, stripped of any coherence or logic. [...] The body [appears] broken, asymmetrical, disarticulated, unstructured, out of kilter, most often supported in an unstable manner by the feet [...]. Permanence is only to be found in the body's perpetual instability and imbalance, risking a decisive downfall at any moment, yet, as if by some miracle, never falling.[1]

The Caribbean being has been constructed through disorder out of existential necessity. Caribbeans know how to make inconsistency consistent, how to stabilize instability, transform disharmony into harmony or render paradox, ambivalence, and contradiction logical. This mode of existence symbiotically melds two [...] states of being: the unstable being and the adaptable being.[2]

Anthropologist, dancer, choreographer, and educator Léna Blou has developed a theory that describes the structure of the Guadeloupean dance *Gwoka* as indicative of the nature of Caribbean people – moving through life in recognition of impermanence as a way of life. She describes *Gwoka* as based on improvisation, driven by a constant alternation between rupture (*Bigidi*) with continuity or status quo, and successive adaptation (*Rèpriz*). The body is kept in a state of instability, constantly anticipating a potential fall in order to be able to counteract it immediately, which might appear to some eyes as "a body out of control."

In Blou's line of argumentation, I kept misunderstanding her assertion that the Caribbeans' ability to *Bigidi* was only developed as a strategy to cope with "shock moments" that interrupted their permanence – such as the imposed control and domination of colonial powers and their aspirations for universalism – and to adapt to the thereby produced new reality. I have failed to recognize, however, that she in fact describes the Caribbean nature as continuously being confronted with change – for example through natural disasters, which have historically affected the Caribbean particularly often due to their geographic and geological location – and permanence as a condition does not exist per se, except as permanent impermanence.

It becomes clear that the binary thinking that renders continuity as contrary to impermanence, and that keeps guiding my reading, simply does not apply here. My colleague Alya Sebti spoke about the "adaptability to the chaos that is life"[3] instead of the adaptability to the chaos that interrupts life. So, the adaptation is not considered a momentous coping mechanism but rather a state of being, dancing, and thus moving through life. So, within this context, the notion of control cannot be understood as a strategy to maintain permanence, making clear that we must deconstruct the understanding of, and therefore the relationship between, chaos and order, and balance and imbalance, which Western thinking proposes as universal.

In her description of the way of moving through life or *mode of existence*, as she describes it – constantly improvising/adapting to ever-changing circumstances – Blou brings together two categories that are by definition theoretically contradictory according to Western thought – stability versus instability, and consistency versus inconsistency. By transforming one part of the opposite-connoted pairs of terms into an adjective or verb to describe the other as a noun, such as "stabilize instability" or "consistent inconsistency," Blou creates an interim solution to dissolve the assumed dichotomy. In both my way of describing the situation and Blou's interim solution, our linguistic means are symptomatic and reflective of our epistemologies. This says much more about the system of thought and its inherent compulsion to classify than about the object itself. A lack of vocabulary shows that language is the tool par excellence for human beings to organize the world: Language categorizes, differentiates, and determines our thinking, what can be thought, and how. It organizes the world by forcing it into schemata and binary structures.[4] The linguistic approach to the world is the basis of any system of differentiation.[5]

Writer and activist Gabriela Jauregui argues, however, that language is not just a passive product of a social system and its way of thinking. By inventing new expressions, different spellings or new ways of expressing things – by creating some chaos in the familiar – and actively using them, even if this is at times met with some rejection and resistance from some sides, as can be seen in current debates on gender-inclusive language, for example, a change in thinking and understanding can be brought about in the long term.[6] Language does not only represent real processes – it carries a performative potential as it can also actively shape and influence them.[7] It is not a question of resisting given rules, but of understanding them as dynamic and finding a playful way of dealing with them – using them in *Bigidi*. Blou's way of using the terminologies makes that very clear.

Returning to *Gwoka* and the notion of control as a strategy to maintain permanence: looking through the eyes of a mind engrained in Western thinking, I see where the association with drunkenness and there-fore the impression of the body being out of control comes from. On close inspection of the dancers during the *swaré-léwòz*[8] on the last evening of the *Invocation*, however, I could observe that moving according to a prescribed order in the spirit of permanence is in fact more fragile and more easily disrupted than constantly adapting to new circumstances without a guiding principle. The latter asks for much more physical control and focus, and nothing can easily throw you off track anymore. From this point of view, we are still surprised that the Western aspiration toward permanence and understanding of adaptation as a strategy to return to it is defended with so much violence, as it is much more doomed to fail.

Taking another angle on reconsidering the understanding of and thus the relationship between chaos and order, balance and imbalance, but staying within the realm of Western thought, I would like to draw on philosophical reflections on the concept of the "constitutional state of emergency." In democratic states, citizens' fundamental rights are regu-lated by a constitution. The government's duty is to defend and guarantee these rights. The political state of emergency is an instrument of state crisis intervention enshrined in the constitutions of many such states.[9] It allows for the shifts of powers within the institutional structure of the constitution in favor of the government in the event of extraordinary conditions – e.g. a terrorist attack, a natural disaster, or an attempted political coup.[10] These conditions are associated with disorder and rhetorically to chaos. In political theory, "chaos" is equated with insecurity and violence and must be countered with greater regulation to restore order. The political state of emergency is an exceptional legal situation in which a government suspends existing law and authorizes the use of state force – the state can repeal parts of the constitution and suspend civil rights or the right of parliament to pass laws – in order to regain control and restore so-called order. Paradoxically, it is a law that suspends its own order to guarantee order. Philosopher Giorgio Agamben describes the "legal state of emergency as a threshold of indeterminacy between democracy and absolutism."[11] The law, conceived as an emergency brake to guarantee freedom and equality, turns out to be their actual cancellation.[12]

Drawing on Agamben, who described "the state of emergency [...] not as the chaos that precedes order, but the situation that arises from its cancellation,"[13] Friedrich Weißbach sees the autocratic decision of a government to suspend constitutional rights as the actual manifestation of chaos. In his explanations, he then distinguishes between chaos and exception (in relation to order and rule) by understanding chaos, in contrast to exception, not only as a negation of the rule, but as an absolute non-rule. Chaos must therefore be understood beyond the rule-exception dualism and thus as something not determined per se.[14] Because the state of emergency defies, and not simply negates, the previous order, it opens alternative and unpredictable options for action. My point here is not to praise the "crisis-induced expansion" of the executive powers of the political state of emergency, of course. I merely implement it as a tool to analyze the legal situation in order to deconstruct the binary understanding of concepts such as order-chaos, permanence-instability.

> Reflecting on chaos reveals the human-made nature of all social and political systems and makes it immediately clear that things could always be different [...].[15]

Contrary to any tendency to naturalize certain power and social structures, chaos can in fact be understood as a political elemental force that renders structures to be variable through and through. Interestingly, this consideration, derived from the logic of a legal system rooted in Western thinking, brings us back to my considerations on adaptation as a state of being, rather than a momentous coping mechanism to return to permanence (as opposed to chaos). So again, chaos is the openness to the process itself.[16] In this sense, the nature of the *Gwoka* and the Caribbeans can be understood as essentially chaotic, too. As I described, it does not strive to follow a predetermined order, to balance imbalance and to pursue permanence. The essence of the dance and nature of being is to be non-form. Accordingly, this form of being and dancing cannot be met with binarily connoted pairs of terms such as stability and instability or chaos and order. The potential fall threatened in the title of the event *Invocation* #2 Guadeloupe: *Bigidi mè pa tonbé!* is therefore in fact an impossible consequence of acting in *Bigidi*. Thus, let us be fearless in inventing other ways of using our words, or even create different ways of expressing ourselves – using our language in *Bigidi* to totter in "chaos that is life" and of which we are an active part of, instead of a reacting entity.

75

1		Léna Blou, "Totter, but Never Fall! The Feint of Time, the Wandering of the Body, and the *Ambigidité* of the Caribbean Being," in Olga Schubert and Eric Otieno Sumba (eds.), *O Quilombismo: Of Resisting and Insisting. Of Flight as Fight. Of Other Democratic Egalitarian Political Philosophies*. Berlin: HKW, 2023, pp.84-85.
2		Ibid., pp.88-89.
3		Text "On Circle, Alignment and Bouncing Back" from this publication.
4		Zoë Herlinger, "Sprache und Chaos — Ambiguität und Paranoia," in Miriam Amin, Elisabeth Niekrenz, and Friedrich Weißbach (eds.), *Chaos. Zur Konstitution, Subversion und Transformation von Ordnung.* Berlin: Berliner Wissenschafts-Verlag, 2018, pp.17-28.
5		Miriam Amin, Elisabeth Niekrenz and Friedrich Weißbach (eds.), 2018, op. cit., p.7.
6		Gabriela Jauregui, "Herramientas desobedientes," Gabriela Jauregui, *TSUNAMI.* Mexico City: Sexto Piso, 2018, p.91.
7		Zoë Herlinger, 2018, op. cit., p.17.
8		The *swaré-léwòz* served as a safe space of communion for enslaved people. It is not a physical space but is rather defined by the spontaneous formation of an empty area that only assumes consistency in its sacralization through human presence.
9		The term "state of emergency," or Ausnahmezustand, does not exist in the German constitutional system. The term is too strongly characterized by the events of the final phase of the Weimar Republic (1918-1933), when the state of emergency became permanent and the parliamentary system had to give way to the dictatorial power of the Reich President. See Birgit Schäfer, *Das Recht des Ausnahmezustands im Rechtsvergleich*, Research Service of the European Parliament (Brussels, 2020). Available at www.europarl.europa.eu/RegData/etudes/IDAN/2020/651938/EPRS_IDA(2020)651938_DE.pdf. Accessed on: 2025.
10		Matthias Lemke, "Was heißt Ausnahmezustand?," in Mathias Lemke, *Ausnahmezustand. Theoriegeschichte - Anwendungen - Perspektiven.* Wiesbaden: Springer VS, 2017, p.2.
11		Giorgio Agamben, *Ausnahmezustand.* Frankfurt am Main: Suhrkamp, 2004, p. 9. In English: *State of Exception,* trans. Kevin Attel. Chicago: University of Chicago Press, 2005.
12		Friedrich Weißbach, "Chaos und Ausnahmezustand," in Miriam Amin, Elisabeth Niekrenz and Friedrich Weißbach (eds.), 2018, op. cit., p.123.
13		Ibid., p.121.
14		Friedrich WeißbachIbid., 2018, op. cit., p.121.
15		Ibid., p.138.
16		Ibid.

Kalanjé

Geordy Zodidat Alexis

Performance in collaboration with
Joane Etheart, holistic practitioner,
dancer, and choreographer, held during
Invocation #2 on December 7, 2024.

Experimentation with *Fwotman* and *Bigidi*,

Traversing these elements, evoking the writing of new codes in a space of another time. *Fwotman* is a holistic medicine used by my Caribbean ancestors. It enables the healing of the three bodies: physical, mental, and spiritual.

I start from Padjanbèl because this dance has a very strong anchoring. The basic step, the *kalanjé*, favors a movement of the body from the outside inward.

Bringing what is outside back inside, as if to reclaim it in order to digest it.

I perceive the concept of *Bigidi* as a long path toward healing the wounds linked to the plantation.

It is precisely because the disorders persist that healing is not yet complete.

I see the need to understand the cultural heritage of this island where I was born as the sowing of a land.

Bigidi is a way of life. In my view, it is an initiation into the understanding of who we are, we the people of Caroucaera – Cibuqueira. It is an introspection, a starting point.

I am truly interested in the healing of the human being. Man is part of the universe and, in fact, he is a universe unto himself.

Becoming aware of what we have and who we are, in my view, is not an end in itself.

Understanding why we have this or that, and where what constitutes us comes from, has a more essential character.

The barriers around Guadeloupe are psychological.

Claiming rights cannot be a state of stability or a way of life. It is an integral part of a process.

What lies beyond this state of claiming? What is this process?

Codification. Reinvention. Evolution.

79

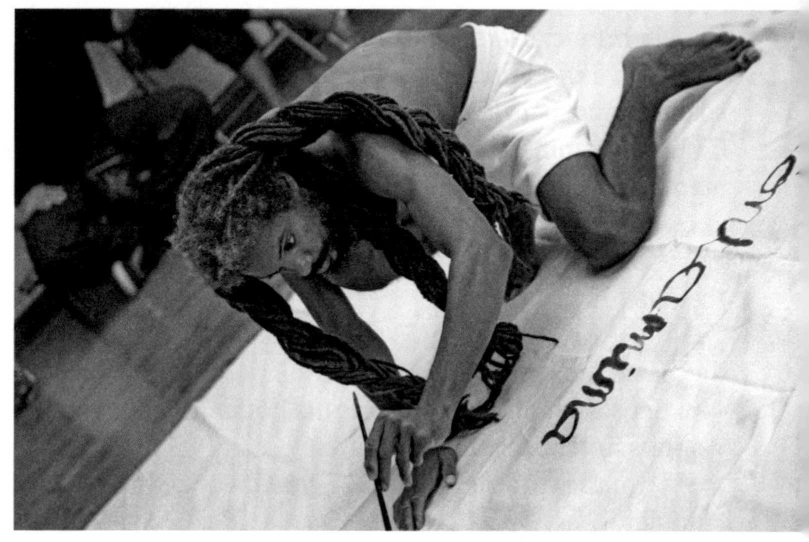

© Philippe Hurgon / Fundação Bienal de São Paulo

Goudoum Takatou Katak Ta Goudoum Takatou Katak Ta Je lis Ka
Goudoum Takatou Katak Ta Goudoum Takatou Katak Ta Je lis La
Goudoum Takatou Katak Ta Goudoum Takatou Katak Ta Je lis Nje
Goudoum Takatou Katak Ta Goudoum Takatou Katak Ta Énergie
Goudoum Takatou Katak Ta Goudoum Takatou Katak Ta Non
Goudoum Takatou Katak Ta Goudoum Takatou Katak Ta Extérieure
Goudoum Takatou Katak Ta Goudoum Takatou Katak Ta

I see the step. Movement of the body. From the outside inward.
Sensation of the hands of this body inhabited by its lineage.
     A conscious vehicle. Ancestrality.
I am the experience seeking the balance that makes symmetry visible.

Goudoum Takatou Katak Ta Goudoum Takatou Katak Ta Ka
Goudoum Takatou Katak Ta Goudoum Takatou Katak Ta Bula
Goudoum Takatou Katak Ta Goudoum Takatou Katak Ta Ka
Goudoum Takatou Katak Ta Goudoum Takatou Katak Ta Buladjèl
Bigidi Bagada Bugudu Begede Bogod

On Circle, Alignment and Bouncing Back

Alya Sebti

Humanity as a practice serves as a guiding philosophy for this edition of the Bienal de São Paulo. The four *Invocations* prior to the exhibition explore how each space and its situated practices reflect a conjugation of humanity.

After the first *Invocation*, centered on the practice of deep listening and active reception in Le 18 and Dar Bellarj in Marrakech, we held a second *Invocation* inspired by the *Bigidi mè pa tonbé*, conceptualized by the researcher and choreographer Léna Blou in Lafabri'k, the cultural center she created in Les Abymes, a neighborhood in Pointe-Pitre, on the Caribbean island of Guadeloupe.

The *Bigidi's* rhythm is punctuated by three moments, and I believe each one could be seen as a verb to conjugate humanity: First, *faire Lawond* acts as a call to create a circle; the dance of balance within imbalance is a second element; and finally, *Rèpriz* is the fundamental philosophy of bouncing back.

Faire Lawond, Creating the Circle

The first morning we gathered at Lafabri'k for the beginning of this *Invocation*, and Léna Blou laughed as she announced, "*Ici on est en Bigidi*! We are here to improvise, to help each other, so let's all grab a chair and create a circle. When we make a circle, we make humanity."

As simple as that, the tone was set.

There is indeed something about circles.

A circle has no beginning and no end. It holds an infinite number of all possible geometric figures. In Islamic architecture for instance, the circle is a symbol of unity and the division of the circle into regular segments is the ritual starting point for many traditional patterns. There is a mystical circularity of shapes and movements in nature: stars, celestial objects, loops, drops, ripples of water, tides, and waves directed by the rhythms of the moon. A circularity of rhythms inherent to nature in echo chambers with the circularity of time.

Telling stories to people sitting in a circle is a familiar practice in many cultures around the world including the Halqa, a Moroccan theatrical tradition; the Agora, the central marketplace and meeting point in ancient Greece; or the Arabic Jamaa, or gathering. Everyone sits equidistant from the shape's center, claiming equal importance to access the performance. There is no hierarchy in receiving or listening in a circle.

Entering a communal circle is often seen as a ritual, acknowledging the space and the community gathered. There are codes of respect before joining the circle: One doesn't simply open or infiltrate it. It requires reflection, and most of all, deep listening to understand

83

the rhythms as to when to act. Creating a circle is a society in the making, a vital communal practice. That's why Léna Blou says that when we make a circle, we make humanity. The circle acts like a membrane to protect its people. In that space of trust and intimacy, people can invent, create and rewrite their humanity.

As Patrick Chamoiseau narrates:

> To consider this poetics (which I inhabit, which inhabits me, which circulates a little in what I write), the best is to open a *la-ronde* (in Creole: an *lawond*), as in the tradition of West Indian evenings. The old *la-ronde* consisted of an assembly around a guy who was going to express a breath of existence: dancing or giving voice. [...] A *la-ronde* was a creative space. [...] We couldn't find a better place in the world to share what we carry within ourselves, so...[1]

First a circle is formed. Then the drum starts, followed by the chanting and clapping. The first dancer enters the circle and creates *Le souffle du monde* [the souffle of the world], as Blou puts it. The breath of creation inherent to humanity.

The circle becomes this crucial space to create; one of solidarity, synergy, interconnectedness. One that welcomes trust and vulnerability. In Blou's approach, the circle is where the individual becomes part of something larger, a collective rhythm where each person entering *la-ronde* has the power to redefine and reinvent their alphabet and compose the score of their existence.

It reminded me of the circle we experienced for the first *Invocation* in Marrakech, during a Hadra, the Sufi trance ritual. The power of chanting and music was harnessed to create a space of collective unity. One would enter the circle in a profound act of trust and surrender, carried by the collective breath and interwoven energies.

Both in Hadra and in the practice of *Bigidi*, the power of music serves as an act of gathering energy. The repetitive, rhythmic chanting and music are an embodied invitation to join the movement. It calls to us, asking us to deeply listen to and have faith in the rhythm, to feel the energy of the group, and to enter in communion with the whole.

The similarity stops at this moment to take two different routes. If the deep listening in the Hadra ritual leads towards a complete surrender to the call necessary to enter a state of trance, the deep listening in the *Gwoka/Bigidi* leads to taking back control of the narrative thanks to the key tool of improvisation.

To continue with Patrick Chamoiseau's thread in *Le Conteur, la nuit et le panier* [The Storyteller, the Night, and the Basket]:

> Dancer, tanbouyé, singer, and storyteller improvise above all. Improvisation completes an individuation by making it attentive to other improvisations, other individuations. This attention (let's say this jazz spirit) is a solidarity very different from that established by the "totalitarian communion" of the old communities. Individuation is the potential basis of a "non-totalitarian communion." Of an unusual exchange between the "I" and the "we," the intimate and the common.
>
> By what process?
> By the appearance of the "person."[2]

It is the improvisation that enables the person and her creative process to emerge. Improvisation is a key to approaching this second movement of humanity in the *Bigidi*: *"danser l'équilibre dans le déséquilibre"* as Léna Blou would say, dancing the balance in the imbalance.

Dancing Balance within Imbalance

When Blou gave a workshop on the *Bigidi*, she said, "Imagine you had way too much rum to drink, then stand up and start dancing. That's the *Bigidi* move, totter but never fall." It's about adaptability to the chaos that is life. There is a *Bigidi* way to apprehend balance: It is through imbalance, an adaptability to align with life's constant movements.

Only circles can hold space for imbalance. Squares simply can't, they are just too rigid. One is invited to dance within the circle, to embrace the chaos of being human. The circle provides the space for us to inhabit the disarray, as the fabric of existence itself. In this space, one learns to dance with imbalance, surrendering to its flow, knowing that we are held within the collective energy. As Blou puts it, the body reinvented its dance to reinvent its humanity.

Règpriz

"Nous avons le droit de trébucher, mais pas de tomber, c'est ça la Règpriz" one can totter, but never fall.

Règpriz is the third and last movement of the *Bigidi*, and I believe it is a fundamental lesson. It's the moment when one creatively bounces back into a rhythm, position, and alignment within chaos. According to Blou, it is "this very moment, the ultimate point of equilibrium, momentum."

The bounce-back dynamics is the *Rèpriz* in the *Bigidi.*

One can stumble, but still trust the circle. One has to listen to the rhythms and movements to be able to improvise within them, dance with discord, and find alignment within, so as to be able to rebound.

As Blou puts it so well, *Bigidi* is a Caribbean key to approaching the future. A "philosophy of the dynamic of rebound." Staying in movement and listening in order to improvise, to find alignment within the imbalance and to take back the narrative to create one's own movement within. At a moment in which society is paralyzed by fear of the unknown, driven by political fragmentations and climate change, *Bigidi* is a fundamental lesson to meet the challenges of our future realities. Because creativity can carve out spaces to reinvent humanity, we won't let catastrophes define us. We would rather learn to dance around them and keep on creating spaces to breathe.

I would like to share with you my interpretation of a magistral moment of *Rèpriz* in the poem of one of the most outstanding voices of Caribbean literature: the poet and visual artist Frankétienne. In his poem "Mûr à crever" [Ripe to the Point of Bursting], there is a moment in which he reclaims control of the catastrophes falling upon him. In the last part: *"C'est alors que je deviens orage de mots crevant l'hypocrisie des nuages et la fausseté du silence."* "It is then that I become a storm of words, piercing the hypocrisy of the clouds and the falsehood of silence." He refuses to let catastrophes overtake him, the creative act of writing is his scream to define his rhythm and to take back the direction of his own story, a storm of words to become the human he decides to be. Creativity to carve out again and again glimpses of hope in humanity.

Every day, I use the dialect of crazy cyclones. I speak of the madness of contrary winds. Every evening, I use the patois of furious rains. I speak of the fury of overflowing waters. Every night, I speak the language of hysterical storms to the Caribbean islands. I speak of the hysteria of the sea in heat. Dialogue of cyclones. Patois of rains. Language of storms. Unfolding life in a spiral. Fundamentally, life is tension. Toward something. Toward someone. Toward oneself. Toward the point of maturity where the old and the new, death and birth, are unraveled. And every being is partly fulfilled in the search for its double. A search that is almost confused with the intensity of a need, a desire, and an infinite quest. Dogs pass by I have always been obsessed with stray dogs they bark at the silhouette of the woman I am pursuing. After the image of the man I seek. After my double. After the rumor of fleeing voices. For so many years. It seems like thirty centuries. The woman has left. Without drums or trumpets. With my out-of-tune heart. The man has not reached out to me. My double is always ahead of me. And the unbolted throats of the nocturnal dogs howl terribly with the sound of a broken accordion. It is then that I become a storm of words bursting through the hypocrisy of the clouds and the falseness of silence. Rivers. Storms. Lightning. Mountains. Trees. Lights. Rain. Wild oceans. Carry me away into the frenzied marrow of your joints.[3]

1   Patrick Chamoiseau, *Le Conteur, la nuit et le panier.* Paris: Edition Seuil, 2021, p.5.

2   Ibid., p.186.

3   Frankétienne, *Mûr à crever.* Port au Prince: Éditions Mémoire, 1995.

An Sé

Anaïs Verspan and Dory Sélèsprika

Performance held during *Invocation #2* on December 6, 2024.

For the *Invocation,* I moved my studio to Lafabri'k. I spent all my time researching and developing a unique and creatively fertile painting methodology.

I live in the north of Grande-Terre, more precisely in Le Moule, surrounded by sugar cane fields. It is from this geographical environment that I give rise to an aesthetic and empirical cultural manifestation. From the cut to the artist's studio, sugar cane becomes a "muse".

It is a proposal to reappropriate and sublimate the semantic fields related to the cultivation of sugar cane.

It is not an aesthetic quest, but a search for the creative experience that leads me to a candid, true, and free pictorial gesture.

All photos: © Philippe Hurgon / Fundação Bienal de São Paulo

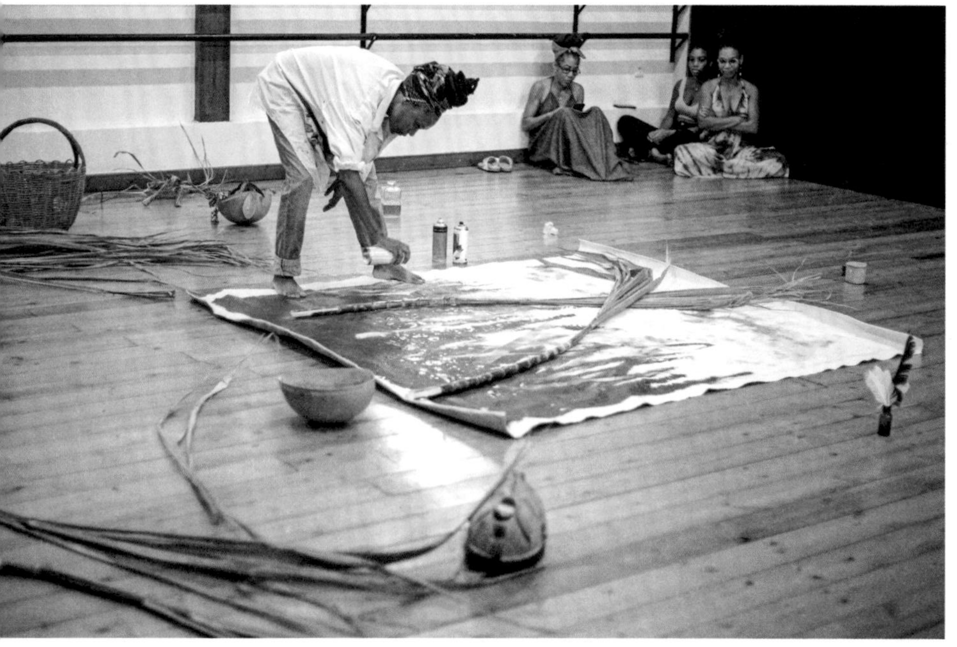

DORY SÉLÈSPRIKA_ poet, slammer

In the past, devalued and devaluing for those who used it, the Guadeloupean language was able to reclaim and regain its place in the daily lives of the inhabitants of Guadeloupe.

Like many other artists before me, I use the Creole language as a liberated force, in response to the title of linguist Dany Bébèl Gisler's work *Langue créole, force jugulée* [Creole Language, Repressed Force], published in 1976.

I propose a new kind of Guadeloupean poetic writing, in which language is conjugated in all tenses and with all people in order to challenge all layers of society. Through my voice, I apprehend space-time: I declare and declaim my texts articulating them in all tones, interpreting the Creole, French, and English languages, languages of yesteryear mixed with urban vocabulary, all tinged with African, American, and Caribbean poetic, rhythmic, and melodic influences (QR Code below).

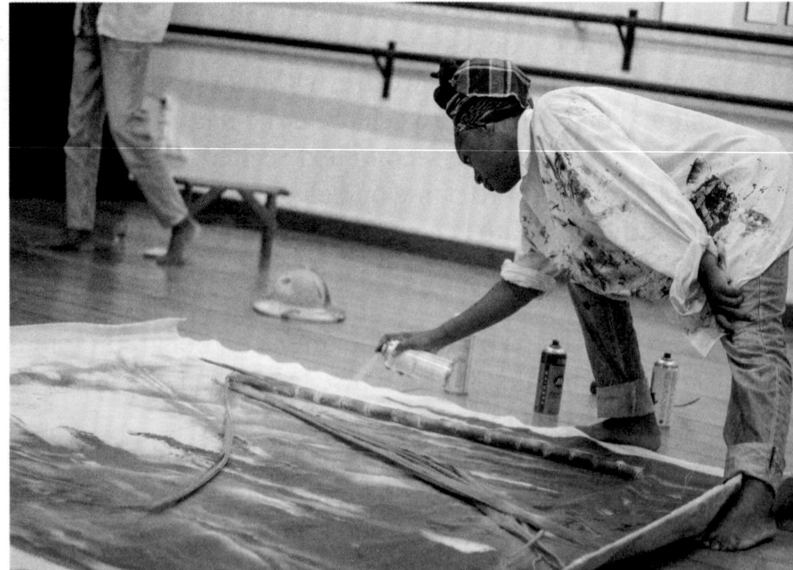

Playlist

MASKS

Have you ever seen eyes closed
Masks you've seen though must be changed

Have you ever heard spoken breathes
Old men's words
Have you ever heard the wind blow
Women's native tongue flow

Have you ever worn soul clothes
Eaten soul food, good for thoughts

Have you ever followed lines,
Ever read history rock inscribes

Have you ever touched Mother earth
Sown seeds, soul feeds,
Soul food, ebony wood
Open minded window
Let the wind blow

DöRY
From the book of poems *Tan*

"MASKS" is the first text I presented during this *Invocation* at the 36th Bienal de São Paulo. Entirely in English, it invites us to accept and appreciate ourselves as we are, without disguises or masks, and without colonial bias, in order to celebrate the natural elements that surround us.

As with the second text recited, "TOLOMAN," the text invokes our right to name ourselves, to hear our own voices, to assume our authenticity, to accept our differences, with the awareness and will to be a people.

Lavi pa on bòl toloman mé on bòl grenn toloman
Onpakèt ti grenn nwè fèmé adan on kalbas
ka soukré an kadans a lavi
Andidan kon andèwò onsèl voukoum ka rann moun soud
Lè-w ka pran tan kouté, toutbiten annòd

91 (Excerpt from "TOLOMAN")

The Guadeloupean language is not only the marker of an oppressive time, it is also an element of the liberation of speech, of oneself, of one's own voice, rich in lexical heritage and expressions drawn from our experiences and our imagination. The "KABANNÉ" texts are paths where it is possible to sing of hope and imagine "Lavi," a life in Guadeloupe mature enough to *fasadé*, to face itself.

> Annou di Gwadloup kon SAPOTI,
> kon ponm-kannèl yo kyouyi
> Annou di i po'o mòl, i po'o bon
> Annou di i poko pran sik é koulè,
> Annou di zyé a-y poko wouvè
>
> [...]
>
> Annou di on jou nou ké mi,
> nou ké vwè klè nou ké ni lanvi
> Nou ké las di dèmen sé on kouyon
> Nou ké las chofé kabann pou bon
> Annou di sé kabanné nou ka kabanné
> Pitit ka vin gran kabanné sé on tan

(Excerpt from "KABANNÉ")

A Guadeloupe relieved of its stigmas, free to reinvent itself, determined to detoxify its beliefs, to pacify its relations with others, its compatriots, the *nou-menm*, to protect the land, to purify the waters, to breathe clean air in order to project itself elsewhere, towards a future that does not forget its roots.

> An sé flanm, koulè flanbwayan
> An sé boukan pèp an mouvman
> An sé difé lèspwa jennès
> Chaltouné mémwa antan lontan
> An sé van ka soukré lang a vyé-fanm Van ka chanté an pyé
>   banbou
> van ka dansé épi flèch a kann
> An sé siren ka mounyé zèb
> solèy ka kléré chak tigout dlo si fèy
>
> [...]

An sé on lavalas ka chayé pwazon latè pou pirifyé nannan a nonm
An sé ziyanm, malanga, mannyòk, an sé dachin
Sizé, pozé dé plat a pyé a-w é pran rasin
Pas ou ni rasin

[…]

An sé solèy é lalin
An sé lanmè é latè
An sé chalè é fwadi
An sé rasin é niyaj
An sé nonm é fanm
An sé lavi
Lavi Gwadloup

(Excerpt from "NANM A NONM" _TAN)

We put our creations on display, celebrating our own form
of sorority.

We create the instant T in an alternative space-time, like the organization of marronage in the cane fields, that of the *Lawonn*.

A true space of science, the *Lawonn* is a space of resistance, trust, resonance, solidarity and protection, a space of letting go where creative freedom is expressed.

Music, the smell of incense or plants, terracotta or wooden objects are all elements that inspire us, but above all they are markers of our temporality of life and creation in this land of Guadeloupe.

This version of the *Invocation* is not a performance, but a sincere stance of who we are, a deep desire to define ourselves, *AN SÉ*.

Poems: "Tropical King" and "Number"

Edinho Santos

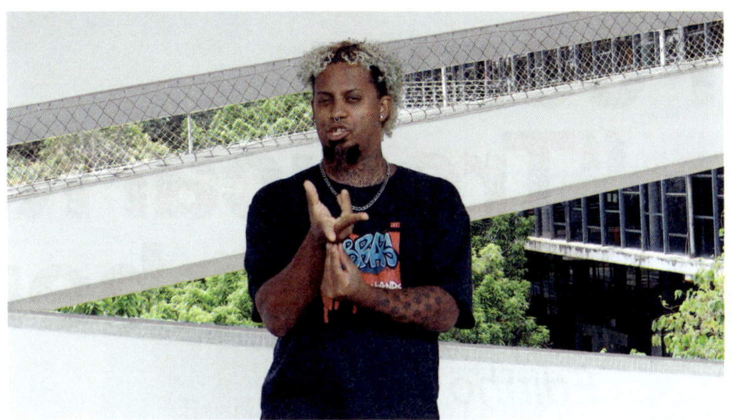

Hello, my name is Edinho and this is my name in sign language.

I'm from São Paulo, I'm in Ibirapuera Park, in the Bienal building.

I'm an artist, a poet. I'm Black, I take part in the Black Movement and I'm also deaf, I communicate in Libras (Brazilian Sign Language), I take part in the movement to value Deaf Culture.

As a poet, I take part in poetry battles and rhyme battles, which are part of the Hip-Hop Movement, so I've been a role model for other deaf people in this area.

Professionally, I have some work experience, I have a degree in pedagogy. I work in the culture industry at Itaú Cultural, mediating and producing events aimed at making deaf culture visible.

I was featured as an actor in a Netflix movie called *O matador* [The Killer], a feature film. I was also invited by the Brazilian rapper Gabriel o Pensador to open his music video with a poem of mine. This video has over 2 million views. This milestone is very important for giving visibility to a Black deaf person like me.

I'm grateful and happy for the opportunity to be in this publication.

Performance
documentation

Tropical King

On my head I wear a beautiful crown
With a presence, imposing
I am Brazilian
Fruit of its fertile lands
The richness of the tropical climate
Fragrant by nature
But when I'm taken from the soil
My thorns can hurt
They are my defense
From so many attacks and negative words
They want to bring me down but I'm strong,
They can judge me but they can't affect me
I have my protection
But just get closer, pay close attention
You'll discover that my essence has a sweet taste
Inside I already feel perfect, I know it
I'm the pineapple, the king

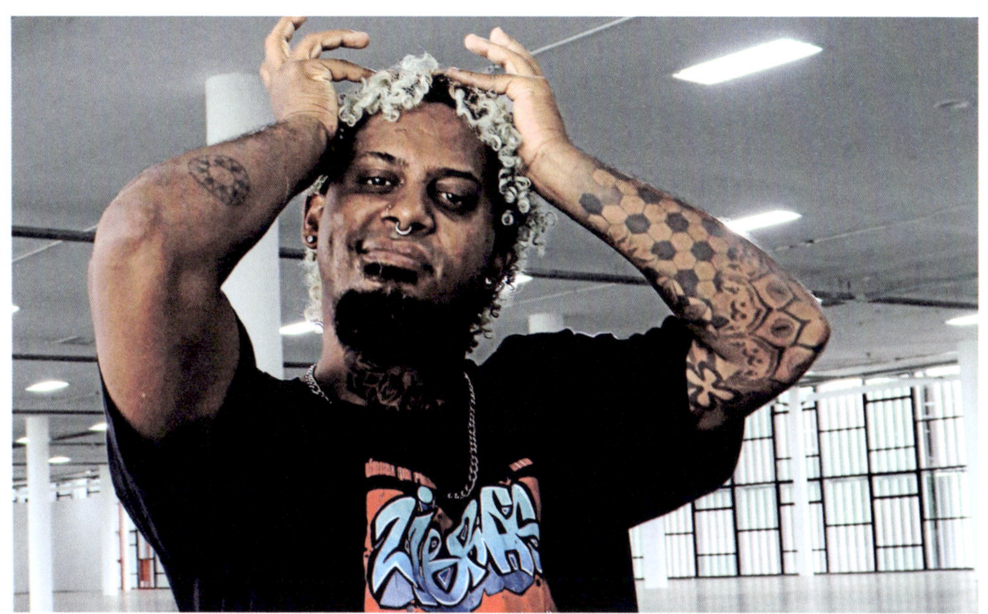

Performance
documentation

Number

We grow up with this lesson
They talk a lot about the number 666
If you do something bad, the devil appears, the dog
You feel that fear, you're uneasy
I tried to behave, I couldn't forget it
If I get into trouble, 666 will appear
Afraid, walking down the street,
Waiting for something to happen.
And as incredible as it may seem, life goes on as normal
666 never did any harm!
I'm Black and deaf
And to be honest, I'm really afraid of another number
Do you want to know which?
If my health gets bad, if I get sick
There's the ambulance number, the one with the red light
They take me to hospital when my health is bad
There's no accessibility there, no Libras, who can explain it to me?
The doctor who will see me later
He gets everything wrong, communicating is complicated
I'm afraid of number 192
But I'll tell you about another, worse number
And I'm much more afraid of that one
Do you know what it is?
I'm Black and deaf
They arrive in a police car, tell me to stop and I won't hear them
One simple action and they grab my hand
I can't communicate anymore
Let go of my hand! Let me speak!
I'm serious, I'm being very honest
The number 666 does nothing
The real devil is 190[1]

1   192 (EMS) and 190 (Police) are Brazilian emergency telephone numbers. [E.N.]

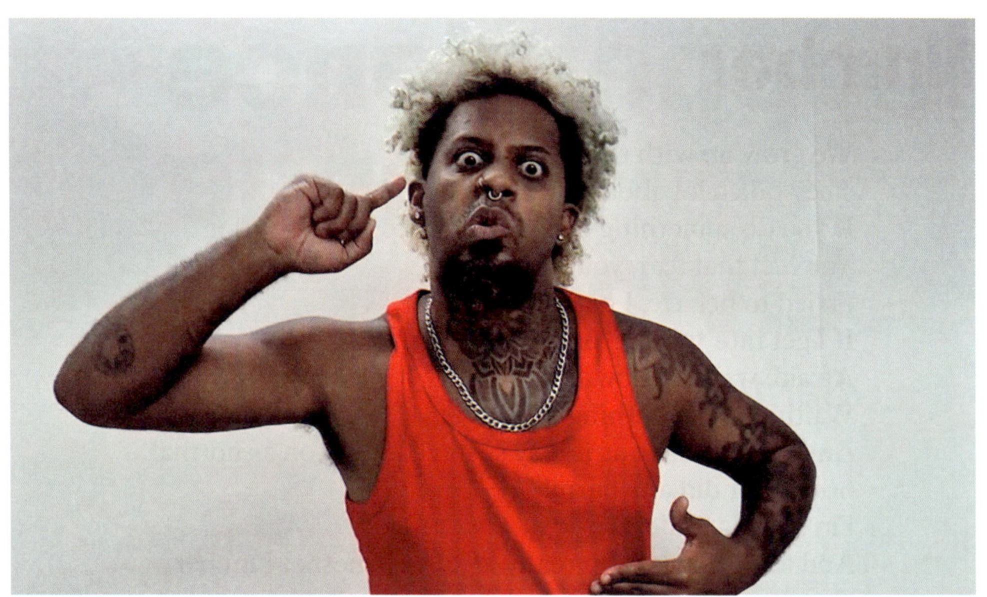

Performance
documentation

Execution Fundação Bienal de São Paulo
Production Ponte Acessibilidade **Concept and Direction** Edinho Santos **Poetry and Performance** Edinho Santos **Artistic Direction** Naiane Olah **Content adaptation** Lívia Vilas Boas e Naiane Olah **Translation and Interpretation** Lívia Vilas Boas e Naiane Olah **Capturing, Editing, Mixing and Finalizing** Miriam Morales **Voiceover** Humberto Bastos **Assembly** Edinho Santos, Lívia Vilas Boas, Miriam Morales e Naiane Olah

Independence Change Living

Santiago Quintana

How do I communicate?

Projection and gesture.
It is necessary to preserve what is meaningful in the gesture while we explore the diverse ways of manifesting it.

Word.

At which time and in which place can the word, voice and gesture turn into a single, same thing?

In spontaneity.

Which space does spontaneity suggest to us when we are three weaving the conversation?

It is necessary to be on the lookout for the echo.

Becoming aware.
The air; the whistle. The transformation of aspiration.
If I whistle outwards, there is a sound.
If I whistle inwards, there is a movement, and also a sound.
The precipice of emptiness: at some point in the presentation, and there must be no one, even with all the bodies present.

The audience disappears.

It has to disappear.

The stare of the spectator is a useful resource–a tool that is used.

"Spect-actors"

The eyes of the spect-actor are hungry. The person performing the scene acts without hunger. Here, balance is given.
        Then, all eyes dance inside the scene. Here there are many doors for the invocation.

The observer acts too.

Doors:

After the doors, there is no more distance between the actor and their observer.
        The mask falls, communication begins, so does the dance, and something breaks. The scene is a collective decision. A consensus.

101

In this invocation, the body is a vehicle:
Of expression.
Of argumentation.
Of exposition.
Of discourse.

How do we depict the echo?
Gestures will be unique, even if the scene is repeated. The role of the spectator can be other than passive. It is a decision. But it will always be reactive.

The spoken words, the unspoken, audiences and lateness do not just happen; they accumulate. The immediate is always happening, and it is the breath that holds it.

Our dance puts the emphasis on the experience of "here and now" – "Now and after."

It tells about the subtle and the visceral.

Invocation.
Presence.
Resonance.
Vulnerability.
Confrontation.
Introspection.
Dialogue.
Rituality.
Impact.
Catharsis.
Echos.

Everyday time, measured, inhabited. Not only time is time.

The body is like a work tool, for example, a clock;

because with it, we can also measure time.
Time is also a metaphor for the scene.

What do you like the most about the stage?
1. NEBULOSITY.

102
2. Reaching 1 after the countdown. It is 1. It is a source of action.

Ruins, decadence and sluggishness
— Look. YOU GET TO THAT CORNER AND TURN RIGHT. Walk on the sidewalk to your right. On the third corner, cross diagonally to the right, and next to the bar "GUAJIRA," on the red door, knock three times. When Ezequiel comes out, tell him: "Ezequiel, give me the keys with the 8-ball."

Life is a constant stage.

Life is the latent stage of our re-evolutions.

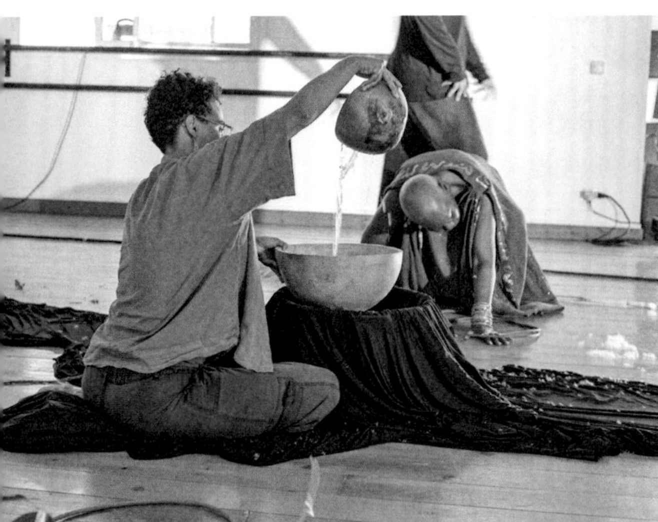

All photos:
Performance by Yane Mareine, Minia Biabiany and Santiago Quintana held during *Invocation* #2 on December 7, 2024.
© Philippe Hurgon / Fundação Bienal de São Paulo

Drawing of the script:
Three come in. There is water.

From the water on the scene, doors will be born. The hands submerge in the water.
The voice becomes dancing, and it transforms at will.

The guide.
All the coexistences form an existence. The self is many.
Cubes not only talk about shape; they also suggest an intention and a position.

Something must happen.
Something is happening.
Something already happened.

How many steps were given since the beginning?
Should we know it?
Where are we now?

Silence.

Flour sings too.
There are multiple voices in the space.
Nobody else knows it.

Even though presence does not know what presence is.
It does not know whether it is here or there.
But here, there is always a new story being born.

The thunder of August rumbles again.
And other doors open.
The song is now another place.
The voices confront each other.

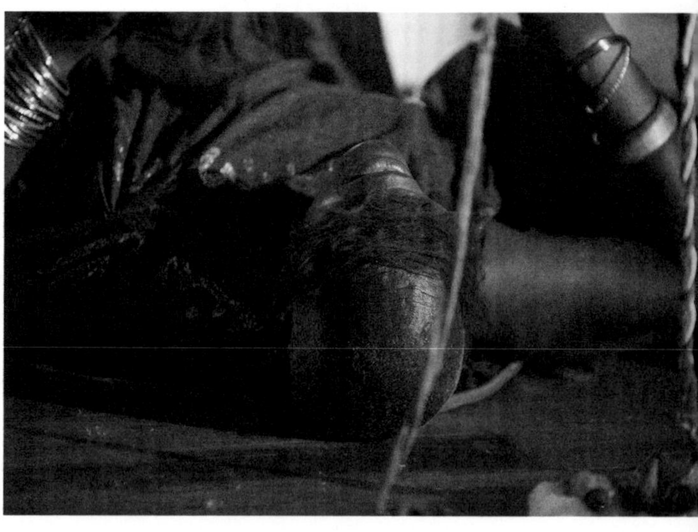

Drops of water on the sensual palms of the hands.
Drops on the forehead of one.
Drops on the forehead of another.

104

One and another are now many.

They are more than a body.

Bodies are measured, and different measures reveal another truth.

The hands meet.
The hands sing.
The hands dance.
The hands follow each other.
The hands leave.

They whistle.

A Body that Weaves

Lidia Lisbôa

Text developed from a conversation between the Fundação Bienal team and the artist on December 10, 2024.

I come from a place, from a family that has no artists. And then, suddenly, I find myself in São Paulo, first working as a housekeeper. This is something I didn't use to say, that I worked as a housekeeper. I worked in an *haute couture* studio, where everything was very lively. Because when I went to work there, I went in to wash, iron, cook, clean, and look after the house.

And suddenly it was also a *haute couture* studio, where I saw people steam flowers, put a flower in a hat, stretch a ribbon. So I started to steam the flowers. I listened to music: Ella Fitzgerald, Billie Holiday, Ray Charles, Charles Aznavour, and so on.

I was always asking for a raise! When the other studio was renovated, I went to work in the new studio. They told me: "Lidia, you're going to work in the studio." And then, as I was kind of, let's say, doing nothing, looking after the studio, I started drawing, putting down my first strokes, making

Lidia Lisbôa
from the series **Casulos [Cocoons]**, 2014-2024
Photo: Henrique Saad
Courtesy of the artist

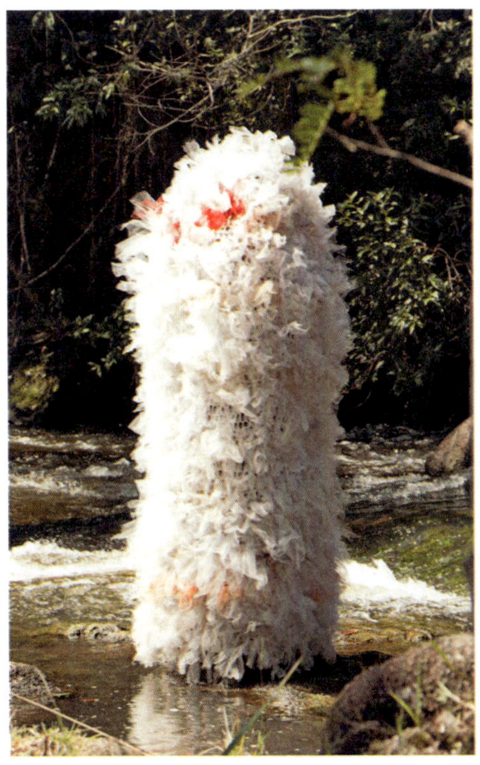

sketches. One day, a client came in, looked at me and said: "Look, you're an artist." I thought: "Oh my God, what now?" Then she looked at me again and said: "You need to find your way, because your way isn't here."

Flowers

When I left the studio at the time, they were very upset with me because they had invested a lot of money and I was also studying. I said: "Look, I work here, but I want to study." So I left. I went to live in a boarding house, I no longer had the privileges I used to have, it became difficult for me. But then I started doing theater. I went from costume design to theater. I met a friend at the time, when there was a Fashion Museum, or rather, the boarding house where I lived became the Fashion Museum, except that, after the Fashion Museum, it also became a brothel, but that's okay. Before the Fashion Museum, I painted my friend S's dresses, dyed them, and did a lot of things. Until she sent me for a test. When I arrived for the test, they said: "You sent me a Black girl."

She said: "You're going to do it because you need to earn that money." To give you an idea, she once put me in the role of the Statue of Liberty, put me in a car and said: "Look, nobody can know you're Black." And she said to the guy: "You're going to put some make-up on her, you're going to thin her nose, and she's going to be the Statue of Liberty," she put me there as the Statue of Liberty. I hate that Statue of Liberty in New York. Because I'd spend hours holding that thing in my hand, you know? So I could earn that money.

Guandu Bean

People say I always tell the same story, but it's just that Uncle Dad, he was a very special uncle in my life. One day – he was my neighbor and he had a camp bed. So I took the camp bed, it was open, I put little guandu bean leaves, one on each side, and put a little flower in the middle.

Then my uncle said to my mother: "Maria, take care of this girl, this girl is different, this girl doesn't fit in with this world." Then my mother said something that I'm not going to tell you, because I'm ashamed of the barbarity of my mother's response. Years later, Uncle Dad came to visit me at home. Uncle Dad was wearing a white t-shirt, a red knitted jacket, jeans, I still remember his jeans, which were blue, very blue, black shoes, and when Uncle Dad came into the house, Uncle Dad turned and said: "Now I understand who that girl was, that girl was an artist, and I didn't know." I said: "Gosh, Uncle Dad, what kind of story is that?" Then he told me about the time I made his campaign bed, with those guandu bean leaves, and he said he was intrigued.

He said there were a lot of guandu bean leaves, and how did I have the patience to put one next to the other, like that, I spent the day doing it, and in the end, a little yellow flower in the middle. That's all I wanted to do. I think that from that moment on, in that memory, that I remember making his camping bed, I was already an artist, and I didn't even know it.

I didn't even know I was an artist, and so I'm 100% an artist. I walk around thinking about what I'm going to make, I eat thinking about what I'm going to make, I dream thinking about what I'm going to make, I'm making things all the time. So, right now I'm doing engraving, but then I go and crochet, then I go and do a *cupinzeiro*, from the *cupinzeiro* I want to do something else, I go around like a shuttle, you know?

As a child, I was already looking after children. I looked after my two siblings, Beth and Marcio. My father brought my dead brother to wash him. I want to make this work, as I said, out of bronze, my dead brother for me to wash.

And then, in the middle of all this, I had a daughter when I was thirteen. Today I have a forty-year-old daughter. Of course it was difficult, but my daughter suckled on Marineuza's teat, my teat, and Dona Norata's teat. She had three tits, a total of six tits. So, what could I say? It's also something that continues, you know? It's like a continuation. I didn't have a childhood. And to this day I'm a mother, I'm a mother of adults. You know? There are people over seventy who come to me for advice. And sometimes I say: "Listen, I'm not going to be a mother, not now." I think it's all part of my work. That's the reason for this crochet, this weave, this knot, this story, these people who come and tell me a story.

Mara Borba, I met Mara Borba[1] in 1992 or 1993, something like that. She and Ismael Ivo,[2] you know? How wonderful, that Ismael Ivo, that sculpture. I went to Santa Catarina to do some performances. I was dressed in a Raul Cortez jacket, then I did a piece, which was a... I did this piece, [shows the piece], I was wearing the jacket and this piece in the sea. I even have the photos. I was in the sea and as the waves came in, they tossed the jacket, the jacket moved, and I was there dancing, doing my performances. When it was over, because I was tired, I bumped into Mara Borba. I said: "Wow, Mara Borba?" Then she looked at me and said: "Lidia Lisbôa, I can't believe it's you. I can't believe it's you." That was at sea, in Florianópolis, near Moçambique beach. I said: "Mara, I can't believe I'm seeing you."

She said to me: "You're doing everything I'd like to do." Then I replied: "But I'm not a dancer, you're a dancer. So stop saying that things don't happen, things happen when you least expect them. You just have to be open. When you're open to it, it comes. Understand?"

You want to travel? I don't have the money to travel. Imagine if I could travel. Do you understand? No, you've already asked, your trip will come. Understand? So that's it, the dancing, the dancing will come.

1	Director, choreographer, composer and performer. Mara Borba was born in Leme (SP) in 1951. She has a degree in drawing and visual arts from FAAP. She studied dance and body expression in Brazil and abroad and chose dance as her profession. She won several awards, including best dancer at the 1st National Contemporary Dance Competition in 1977.

2	Dancer, choreographer, director and curator. He was born in 1955 in São Paulo (SP) and died in 2021 in the same city. He was the first Black director to take over the direction of Balé da Cidade, after a long period of international artistic exposure. He collaborated with the Venice Biennale as dance director from 2005 to 2012 and directed the dance company of the German National Theater in Weimar.

111

Climate Change Impacts, Adaptation and Resilience in the Caribbean: A Narrative in Earth System Balance, Harmony and Resilience

Michelle Mycoo

Conference held during *Invocation #2* on December 6, 2024.

Planet Earth is a living manifestation of nature in harmony and balance. The daily rising and falling of the tides represent a perfect rhythm as is the ritual dance between dawn and dusk when the sun says farewell and welcomes the moon. These cycles are expressions of opposites that balance each other, keeping the cosmos in perfect order, a master class in contrast and harmony, beauty in duality, a perfect balance of this celestial reality.

Humankind, an integral part of nature, has lived on one planet – the Earth – for thousands of years, but the future of humankind will depend on our respect for nature and how we utilize our natural resources. While throughout history consumption of natural resources has been disruptive, we bear witness today of unprecedented changes in temperature, precipitation, droughts, floods and the frequency of extreme events such as tropical cyclones. Climate change – one of the greatest threats to the survival of the human species – is increasingly on the minds of people and governments around the world, as we grapple with unprecedented disruptions to our economies, ecosystems and cultures. The climate crisis knows no planetary boundaries.

Climate Change Impacts and Vulnerability

As geographically special entities, Caribbean islands are among the nations disproportionately at risk from climate change. Although their carbon footprint is small, accounting for less than 1% of global greenhouse gas emissions, they face an existential threat especially if the world experiences an increase in global temperature beyond 1.5 degrees Celsius above pre-industrial averages. "1.5 °C to Stay Alive" was a slogan adopted by the small island states in accordance with the Paris Agreement, which aimed to pursue efforts to limit global temperature rise to 1.5°C and to keep well below 2.0°C above those recorded in pre-industrial times. The 1.5°C target was agreed upon because there was very strong evidence that as the world moved closer to 2°C, the impacts would become much more extreme and some changes could become irreversible.

The Caribbean is experiencing a wide range of climate change impacts, including rising temperatures, heat stress, sea level rise, flooding, drought, storms, and hurricanes.[1] The accelerated melting of glaciers will cause sea levels to rise around island coastlines, drowning ecosystems, flooding urban settlements, and causing saltwater intrusion of freshwater resources found in rivers and aquifers. The impact of sea level change on the settlements and infrastructure on small islands is proportionally greater than on larger land masses, in part due to longer coastlines per unit of land area.[2] The warming of the world's oceans threatens the survival of sensitive ecosystems such as coral reefs, which may die and become less able to protect coastlines from storm surges. Agriculture, fisheries and tourism, the pillars of Caribbean economies, will be affected by the loss of ecosystem services provided by nature. Economies may collapse leaving Caribbean islands with high levels of debt and grinding poverty. In addition, Indigenous and traditional cultures, as well as historic buildings and archeological sites on the Unesco World Heritage List, are at risk if the impacts of climate change continue unabated.

Recent studies report that physical health is a growing concern in the Caribbean as higher temperatures increase the incidence of mosquito-related illnesses such as Dengue.[3] Significant associations with climate-related disasters on the health of populations have been found, as well as significant increases in mental health-related symptoms following Hurricane Dorian, particularly major depression, generalized anxiety or post-traumatic stress disorder among adults, children and medical personnel, some of which persisted for at least six months after the hurricane. When nature's balance and harmony are disrupted by changes in the earth's temperature, there is a chain reaction among ecosystems that negatively impacts economies and people. The natural and human systems are intricately woven into a single tapestry.

Urbanization, the Coastal Zone and Climate Change

For the Caribbean Small Island Developing States, many of our colonial-era capital cities are located in the Low Elevation Coastal Zone (LECZ), coastal areas less than ten meters above sea level that are hydrologically connected to the sea. Approximately 22 million people in the Caribbean live below six meters in elevation.[4] On average, 84% of the region's population lives within 25 kilometers of the coast, and 33% live in low-elevation coastal zones. High concentrations of population, assets, and infrastructure in the LECZ are exposed to flood risks. Based on SLR projections, almost all port and harbor facilities in the Caribbean will suffer inundation in the future.[5]

Tropical cyclone (TC) events associated with ocean warming due to climate change are becoming more intense. The Caribbean has experienced a growing number of Category 5 hurricanes, such as Maria and Beryl, which have destroyed urban infrastructure and buildings. TC Maria in 2017 destroyed nearly all of Dominica's infrastructure, with losses per unit of GDP amounting to more than 225% of the annual GDP.[6] TC Maria in Puerto Rico resulted in more deaths per 100,000 among people living in municipalities with the lowest socioeconomic development.[7] Tropical storms accounted for US\$181.3 billion of the total estimated damages occurring in the Caribbean from 2000 and 2020.[8] Heavy precipitation associated with such extreme events and storm surges have caused severe flooding across many urban settlements, especially those lacking adequate drainage infrastructure and have experienced loss of natural coastal ecosystems such as wetlands, which act as buffers against flooding and erosion. The cost of flood damage in the Caribbean between 2000 and 2020 is estimated at US\$141 billion.[9]

Adaptation Among Caribbean Islands

Adaptation in the Caribbean takes the form of protection, accommodation and retreat. A closer examination of adaptation strategies is necessary to clearly understand which are relevant to the Caribbean context and what the limits of adaptation are.

In the context of planning for urban settlements, some of these adaptation measures include engineering measures, ecosystem-based adaptation, zoning standards, improved building codes and better retrofitting, compact urban form instead of urban sprawl, and less reliance on automobiles to enhance low-carbon urbanization.

Designing with nature in urban areas can help populations cope with the impacts of climate change. Blue-green infrastructure plays a key role in urban planning. Urban green open spaces are the hidden wealth of cities, as they are the lungs of city residents and can help sequester carbon. They include waterfronts, rivers, and other coastal areas, such as wetlands that surround Caribbean cities. Urban landscaping with blue and green belts of trees and parks can also help reduce heat stress and flooding.

Vernacular architecture throughout the Caribbean was designed to cope with the tropical heat. Indigenous populations understood the importance of building high ceilings to keep homes cool. Traditional knowledge informed the design of hip roofs to withstand the high winds associated with hurricanes. Such designs should be incorporated into homes and other buildings to help mitigate the effects of extreme heat.

Protection Measures

In the Caribbean, protection is used to maintain or introduce new defenses that absorb wave energy and minimize coastal erosion and flooding. In Barbados, for example, coastal engineering has been used to protect the more highly developed southwest and west coasts, where erosion is common.

The seawalls built in Georgetown, Guyana, are being used to address coastal flooding and sea level rise. But hard engineering has some disadvantages. For example, seawalls are costly to build and maintain. In addition, while coastal engineering may minimize erosion along some shorelines, it may deprive other areas of sediment, thus disturbing the coast's equilibrium. Furthermore, because seawalls are immobile defenses, they can interfere with natural processes such as habitat migration, which is naturally induced by changes in the sea level. Seawalls can cause coastal squeezing, a process that reduces the area of intertidal habitats such as sandy beaches because these environments are trapped between rising sea levels and immobile, hard defenses.

Ecosystem-based Adaptation

Traditionally, EbA activities, particularly at national and regional scales, have focused predominantly on restoration or conservation of coastal and marine ecosystems (e.g., coral reefs, mangrove forests and seagrass meadows), with less emphasis on the services provided by natural inland forests.[10] However, the inclusion of forests is increasing, in most cases as components of Ridge to Reef projects, and is aimed at integrated watershed management to provide downstream water security, erosion control and ultimately to protect the health of coral reef ecosystems.[11] In addition, mangrove replanting is increasingly being used to defend Caribbean coastlines and reduce land-based pollutants that impact coral reef health. Since the 1990s, artificial reefs have been used in small islands to support reef restoration and reduce beach erosion (e.g., Dominican Republic, Antigua, Grand Cayman, Grenada). They have been successful in reducing the destructive impacts of extreme events, depending on their technical characteristics and the local context.

EbA approaches have many benefits, but also face several challenges and limitations. Biophysical limitations may render some EbA and nature-based solutions ineffective. For example, coral reefs are unlikely to withstand rising temperatures, reducing the effectiveness of coral reef-based EbA options under higher temperature scenarios.[12] Similarly, many other coastal and marine ecosystems, such as mangroves, face severe limitations with increasing sea levels and other climate impacts.[13]

Retreat, Relocation and Resettlement

In situ adaptation options are preferred by most communities over relocation. On the other hand, resettlement – both planned and autonomous – is an adaptation option of last resort due to its high economic and sociocultural costs.[14] Resettlement of households, communities and larger island populations is increasingly discussed in the context of loss and damage when in situ adaptation limits are believed to have been reached. Limited data and research on adaptation limits and transformative adaptation means that policy applications are currently limited.[15]

Adaptation Finance

Caribbean islands affected by extreme events such as hurricanes and floods have raised their voices at the COP meetings to seek adaptation finance to offset loss and damage and to support recovery. In the aftermath of such disasters, they have had to divert funds from development to post-disaster recovery. COP 29 was a major disappointment for Small Island Developing States, as many articulated that the US$ 100 billion pledge from the Global North to the Global South for adaptation expires in 2025, and it took twelve years to finally deliver on this funding promise. There is also uncertainty about whether it will reach the most vulnerable countries. Moreover, it took two weeks of deadlock before a climate finance deal could be reached. The Baku summit agreed that a bare minimum of US$ 1.3 trillion is needed by 2035 (the real figure is likely to be US$ 2 trillion or more). This is in stark contrast to the estimated US$ 5-7 trillion in fossil fuel subsidies that the world's governments each year. Caribbean leaders such as Mia Mottley, Prime Minister of Barbados, have been pushing to transform the global financial system that handles climate finance. Prime Minister Mottley has been a vocal advocate for debt cancellation for countries on the frontlines of climate change, such as island nations. High debt levels have forced many vulnerable countries to spend more on debt than on preparing for climate impacts or providing basic social services. The climate crisis we face today requires more decisive climate action and access to adaptation finance.

Conclusion

Top priorities for the Caribbean region include multidisciplinary efforts to innovate relevant solutions, improve stakeholder engagement, and increase access to climate adaptation finance. "Science is our most powerful instrument to tackle climate change, a clear and imminent threat to our well-being and livelihoods, the well-being of our planet and all its species" (IPCC). Art is an essential medium for communicating scientific knowledge to both communities and decision-makers. The power of the written, visual and performing arts to raise awareness and a call to action.

1   M. Mycoo et al., "Small Islands," in H.-O. Pörtner et al. (eds.), *Climate Change 2022: Impacts, Adaptation and Vulnerability. Contribution of Working Group II to the Sixth Assessment Report of the Intergovernmental Panel on Climate Change.* Cambridge and New York: Cambridge University Press, 2022, pp.2043-2121.

2   P. Nunn and R. Kumar, "Understanding Climate-human Interactions in Small Island Developing States (SIDS)," *International Journal of Climate Change and Strategic Management,* v.10, n.2, pp.245-271, 2018.

3   N. Rise, C. Oura, and J. Drewry, "Climate Change and Health in the Caribbean: A Review Highlighting Research Gaps and Priorities," *The Journal of Climate Change and Health*, v.8, 2022.

4   A. Cashman and M. Nagdee, "Impacts of Climate Change on Settlements and Infrastructure in the Coastal and Marine Environments of Caribbean Small Island Developing States (SIDS)," in *Caribb. Mar. Clim. Chang. Rep. Card: Sci. Rev.,* pp.155-173, 2017.

5   Ibid.

6   D. Eckstein, M. Hutfils and M. Winges, *Who Suffers Most from Extreme Weather Events? Weather-related Loss Events in 2017 and 1998 to 2017.* Germany: Germanwatch, 2018.

7   C. Santos-Burgoa et al., "Differential and Persistent Risk of Excess Mortality from Hurricane Maria in Puerto Rico: A Time-series Analysis," *Lancet Planet. Health*, v.2, n.11, pp.e478-e488, 2018.

8   Central Bank of Barbados, "The Cost of Climate Change for Caribbean Economies," *CBB*, Barbados, 4 Jul. 2024. Available at: www.centralbank.org.bb/news/press-releases/the-cost-of-climate-change-for-caribbean-economies. Accessed on: 2025.

9   Ibid.

10   J. Mercer et al., "Ecosystem-Based Adaptation to Climate Change in Caribbean Small Island Developing States: Integrating Local and External Knowledge," *Sustainability,* v.4, n.8, p.1908-1932, 2012.

11   J. Förster et al., "Climate Change Impacts on Small Island States: Ecosystem Services Risks and Opportunities," in M. Schroter et al. (eds.), *Atlas of Ecosystem Services.* Cham: Springer Cham, pp.353-359, 2019.

12   J. Barkdull and P. G. Harris, "Emerging Responses to Global Climate Change: Ecosystem-based Adaptation," *Global Change Peace Security*, n.31, v.1, pp.19-37, 2018.

13   R. Morris, "From Grey to Green: Efficacy of Eco-Engineering Solutions for Nature-based Coastal Defence," *Glob. Change Biol.*, v.24, n.5, pp.1827-1842, 2018; A. Thomas et al., "Global Evidence of Constraints and Limits to Human Adaptation," *Regional Environmental Change*, v.21, n.3, 2021.

14	K. McNamara and D. Combes, "Planning for Community Relocations Due to Climate Change in Fiji," *Int. J. Disaster Risk Sci.*, v.6, n.3, pp.315-319, 2015; R. N. Crichton, M. Esteban and M. Onuki, "Understanding the Preferences of Rural Communities for Adaptation to 21st-century Sea-level Rise: A Case Study from the Samoan Islands," *Climate Risk Management*, v.30, 2020.

15	A. Thomas e L. Benjamin, "Policies and Mechanisms to Address Climate-induced Migration and Displacement in Pacific and Caribbean Small Island Developing States," *Int. J. Clim. Chang. Strateg. Manag.*, v.10, n.1, pp. T86-104, 2018.

The *Blip* and the *Pi Tak*: Humanity Verbs of the Improbable

Étienne Jean-Baptiste

Conference held during *Invocation* #2 on December 7, 2024.

Introduction: *Blip* and *Pi Tak*, the Syntax of a Reinvented Humanity

The onomatopoeia *Blip* and *Pi Tak* are not merely expressions of sound; they incorporate the *fundamental verbs* of a symbolic grammar born from the fractures of the New World. These sounds, at once spontaneous and collective, reflect a unique anthropological transformation in the colonial Americas. Originating from practices such as the *Martiniquais Bèlè*, they reflect a unique way of reconfiguring humanity in the face of historical violence.

Blip and *Pi Tak*: Symbolic Verbs and Sound Narratives

Because of its incisive brevity, *Blip* symbolizes instantaneity and the capacity for emergence. In the *Bèlè* circle, it marks decisive moments of transition, translating both an individual decision and a collective questioning. *Pi Tak*, on the other hand, carries a deeper and more continuous resonance. It reflects the importance of social bonds and shared rhythms, which are at the heart of Caribbean identity.

These expressions are not simply cultural residues. They "reinterpret the conditions of slavery, not as subordination, but as a space for the invention of the human."[1]

They represent the overcoming of "noise" in humanity. European chroniclers are at the origin of reducing these expressions to noise: "He who plays the big drum beats moderately and slowly; but he who plays the baboula beats as fast as he can, and almost without rhythm, and since the sound he emits is much less than that of the big drum, and very high pitched, *it serves only to make noise*, without marking the cadence of the dance, nor the movements of the dancers."[2] It's actually a form of oral transcription and writing called onomatopoeia that we use in the Afro-Caribbean area to transcribe and decipher musical ideograms.

An illustration in the *Bèlè* circle

On a *Bèlè* night, the *Blip* and *Pi Tak* sounds find their materiality through gestures and interactions in which each participant contributes to a collective narrative of *social manifestos*.

123

1. The Chaos of the New World: The Matrix of Reinvention

An Anthropological Explosion

The *Bèlè: a socio-musical-coreographic system requires an "alternative social grammar."*[3] Born in a context of servitude and plantation, in a form that can be described as Proto-*Bèlè* under the word *Calenda*, it allowed communities to express their collective identity and resist cultural erasur.

2. *Blip* and *Pi Tak*: Structurig Onomatopoeia

2.1 *Blip*: Emergence

Blip is a flash, a sound fragment that marks a decisive moment in the interaction between the dancer, musician, and audience. It reflects "the immediate expression of the present moment in the *Bèlè* circle."[4] This sound punctuates the dancers' transitions or improvisations, offering a space for the unpredictable to emerge.

An Instant Sound Narration

Blip represents incorporated improvisation. Léna Blou adds that "this sound emerges as an interpellation, a flash that disturbs the dynamics of the circle in order to better reorganize them in a new spontaneous order."[5]

2.2 *Pi Tak*: Relational Continuity

Pi Tak, in contrast to the brevity of *Blip*, is a longer sound that evokes resonance and collective continuity. It translates the importance of social bonds and harmony in the *Bèlè* circle. Jean-Baptiste describes it as "a constant reminder of the role of community in cultural reinvention."[6]

3. A Language of Rehabilitation as a Symbolic Space of Unity

The drum, the singing and the dancing come together to erase the artificial boundaries imposed by racialization. These elements embody a collective language in which each participant, regardless of their origin, contributes to a universal and shared memory.

The *seven structuring principles* emerge from this space of improbable unity. *Chantè, Répondè, Bwatè, Tanbou, Dansè, Lawonn,* and *Kadans* constitute the essential pillars of *Bèlè* practices, offering a coherent and dynamic structure to this artistic and social form: *Matrice Bèlè.*

→ The *Chantè* or the execution of a series of themes that qualify the practice.

→ The *Répondè* or enunciation of the themes emitted by the *chantè.*

→ The *Bwatè* (*Boula, foulé*) or game of support in ostinato to determine the genre.

→ The *Tanbou* (*Makè, Koupé*) or formal game of musical structuring singularizing the genre.

→ The *Dansè* or action or bodily movement induced by the genre.

→ The *Lawonn* or *interactive distribution of the dance* within the *assembly* to make it *effective.*

→ *Kadans, Rèpriz,* or the production of energy that characterizes the musical practice.

Damié, Fouytè and *Bèlè*: The Verbalization of a New Humanity

The different forms of *Bèlè*, especially the *Damié*, the *Fouytè*, and *Bèlè* itself represent the pillars of a reinvented humanity. Each of these dances brings a unique grammar to this reaffirmation.

The *Damié*: The Adaptability of Fleeting Identity

The *Damié*, due to its improvised and random nature, reflects the fluidity and adaptability of Caribbean identities. "This dance illustrates how Caribbean communities navigate between tradition and innovation, between heritage and transformation."[7]

The *Damié*, a key fighting dance in the *Bèlè* repertoire, embodies the ability of Caribbean identities to navigate between the constancy of heritage and the need for innovation. Its rhythmic structure and choreography, although codified, are about improvisation and individual interpretation. This flexibility reflects an essential characteristic of Caribbean societies: their ability to adapt to constantly changing contexts.

Fluidity Fragmented Into Fractals

The *Damié* illustrates this "fleeting identity" typical of Creole cultures. "This dance is a metaphor for the journey of identity, where tradition and modernity coexist in the same dynamic."[8] This capacity for integrating new elements while respecting ancestral codes reflects an adaptability that is at the heart of Martinique's cultural practices. The *Damié* constitutes a form of DNA in *Bèlè* or even Martiniquais musical thinking. It presides over the declinations of forms.

The *Damié* is sustained by a characteristic polyrhythm. The drums dictate a rhythmic structure with an improbable base, and the dancers and musicians constantly improvise on the basis of this pattern. This allows for constant reinvention, where each performance becomes unique.

A Typical *Damié* Score

The scores of the *Bèlè tanbou* drum, used for the *Damié*, show a melorhythmic formula derived from the *Takpitakpitak* or *cinquillo* reduced to the 1st, 3rd and 5th sounds of this formula, which is superimposed out of sync on three levels. The *Bwatè* and *Tanbu* are in fact confusing, ambiguous: which of these three superimpositions constitutes the *Tanbu* or *Bwatè*, even though they are made up of the same formula? This *ambiguity* defines the *Damié*. The game of rupture/adaptation translated by the *Rèpriz* determines the random *Tanbu*.

An excerpt from a typical *Damié* score illustrates this structure. In a more elaborate and subtle way, the *Damié* genre is defined by the level of irregular superimposition of the same musical material: 1, 3, 5 of the *cinquillo* superimposed on three out-of-phase levels of *Tak* and *Pi*.

It's the 1/3/5 of the *ti bwa* which is a cultural reference anchored in the musical representations of the people of Martinique. The 5th stroke of the left hand of the *cinquillo* is not played, as it is synchronous and redundant with the 1st stroke of the right hand.[9]

The *Damié* would therefore be the irregular overlapping of the reference cell

Damié

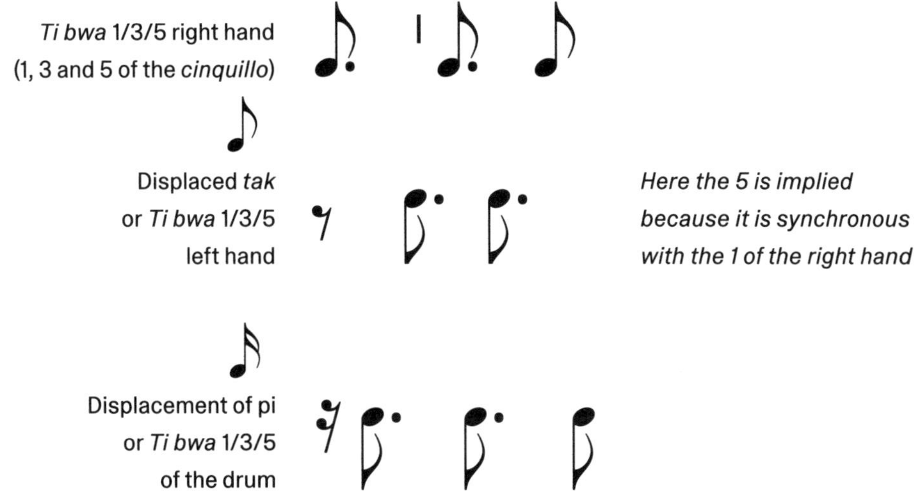

Décalé *Cinquillo* Damié

Ti bwa cinquillo	1			3			5		Reference cycle	♪.♪.♪
	(5)		1			3			Shift of Tak	♪
Tambou Damié		1			3			5	Shift of Pi	♪

The *Fouytè Socialité* of Mutual Aid, a *Rèpriz* from the Chaos of the World

The *Fouytè*, the "dance" of labor, is emblematic of the *Bèlè* repertoire as a symbolic formulation of the advent of post-slavery mutual aid societies. This dance is distinguished by its metered structure, precision, and intensity. Through its movements and collective dynamics, it reflects the capacity of communities to rebuild solid social ties in a context marked by rupture and historical chaos. It is important to note that "this codified dance reflects a collective effort to recreate social ties and reinvent organizational structures."[10]

127

The *Fouytè*

An example of *Fouytè*:

Casérus Emile CD 1970
With Félix Casérus on the drum
Initial rep

WA WA SE MWEN

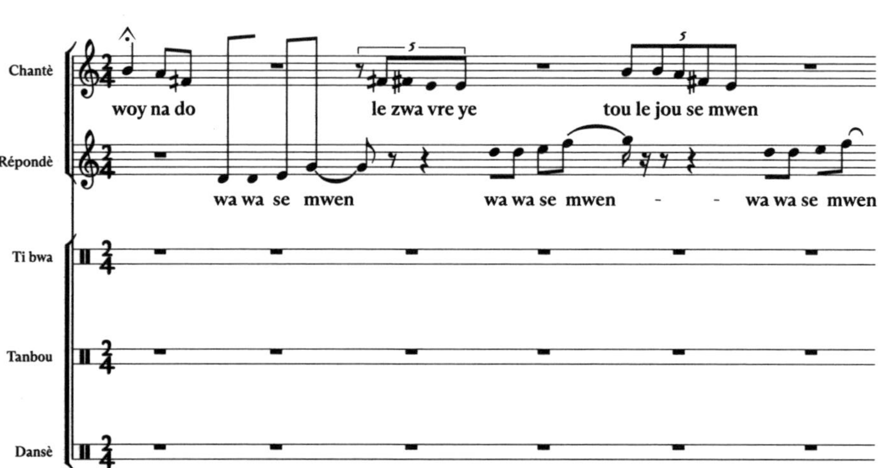

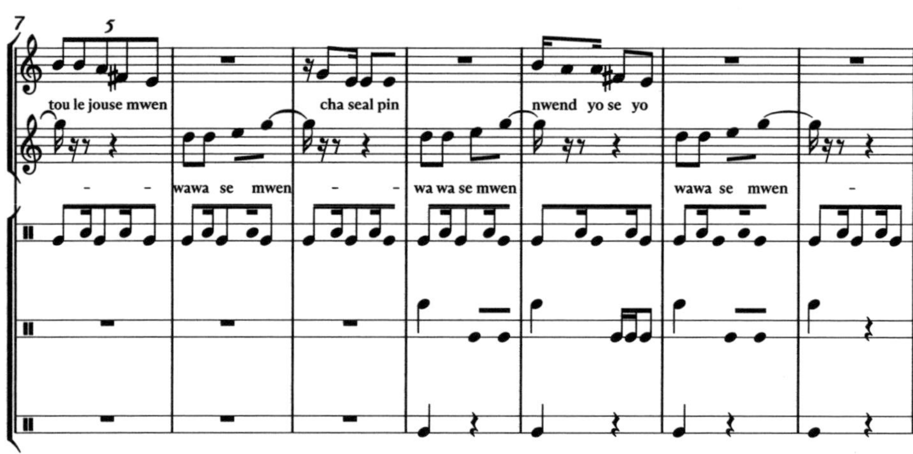

Reconstruction and Social Harmony:
A Choreography of Interdependence

The *Fouytè* "dance" stages a choreography in which the gestures of the farmers or "dancing laborers" are part of a linear dynamic. The *Fouytè* depicts a performance of social cohesion, human values such as solidarity, mutual aid: the entire rural community is in alignment with the laborers, and the cadence of the work is placed into a social order through mutual aid assemblies of musicians. The *Dansè* formalizes and perpetuates the technical culture and organization of work, "ecological" techniques of work and culture, the *Grajé mannyok* in the agri-food sector around the processing of manioc flour, the treatment of cocoa beans, the technique of building huts with mud mortar walls, more recently concrete housing, with heteroclite elements from the "popular" neighborhoods of the capitals.

An Aesthetics of Overcoming

Fouytè also embodies an *aesthetic of overcoming*, where bodies aligned in movement become symbols of resistance and reinvention. Every gesture, every drumbeat translates the ability of communities to transform chaos into harmony: to live together in a community of destiny. Léna Blou formulates this as follows in *Fouytè*: "Bodily energy is a direct response to the uncertainties of the world, a way of rewriting order in disorder."[11]

Bèlè: A Living Grammar of the Polyphony of Expression

Bèlè is an art form in which each participant – dancer, player, singer, and spectator – contributes to a polyphony of expressions. This polyphony reflects the diversity and interconnectedness of roles in Martiniquais society. In effect, each element of the performance, be it the rhythm of the drum, the vocal melody or the dancer's movements, is integrated into a collective harmony. In fact, *Bèlè is a polysemic term*, which firstly is generic, signifying the entire *Bèlè* repertoire with more than a dozen different musical-choreographic genres: the *Bèlè*. Secondly, it designates a specific genre, a type of piece called *Bèlè*. Finally, it is a qualifier to designate any element that has to do with the *Bèlè*: the *Bèlè* night (the performing space), the *Kay Bèlè* (the specific place to hold the *Bèlè* night), the *jan* or *Lawonn Bèlè* (the *Bèlè* community), the *tanbou Bèlè* (the specific instrument for playing the *Bèlè*).

129

Conclusion: An Unlikely, yet Transformative Humanity

The Primordial Verbs of Transformation

The primordial verbs *Blip* and *Pi Tak* conjugate the inversion of the terms of social relations through a symbolic music-choreographic codification.

A Reinvented Humanity
A reminder of the definition of *Bigidi*

"The theory of *Bigidi* or the theory of the harmony of chaos, born of praxis, is formulated, in its axiomatic translation, as a general principle of rupture/adaptation/fluidity, of a phenomenon or a reality. Here, rupture generates an instability whose management must be part of a fluidity understood as circularity. This circularity is conceived as an integration of imbalance, as a law or foundation of adaptation."[12]

The performance of a genre from the *Bèlè* repertoire, such as *Bélia*, is expressed through a *micro Bigidi*, which is expressed through the beat of the *Bèlè* drum and the gestural homology of the dancer.

© Philippe Hurgon / Fundação Bienal de São Paulo

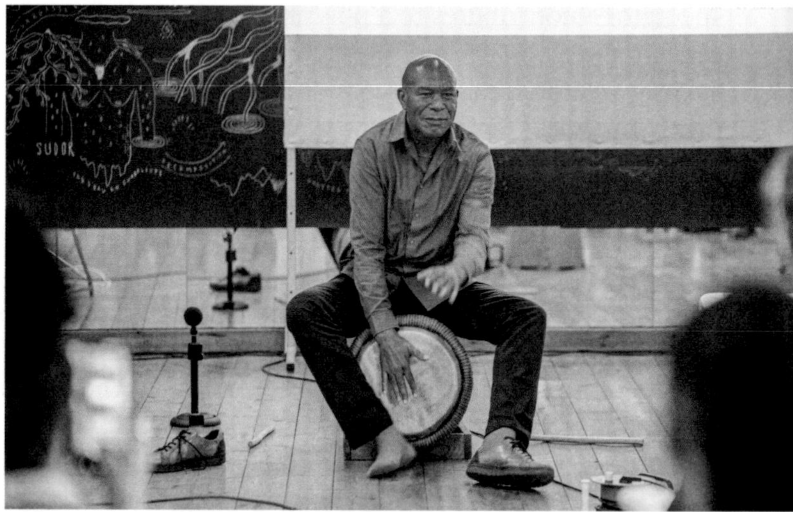

Macro Bigidi

The *principle of inversion* or *tjou pou tèt*, the inconceivable, is conceived in rupture/adaptation/fluidity.

The *Damié anbigité* mentioned above is no stranger to this change in the *Gwoka cinquillo*, which transforms Guadeloupe's humanity into a harmony of oscillations.

Damié

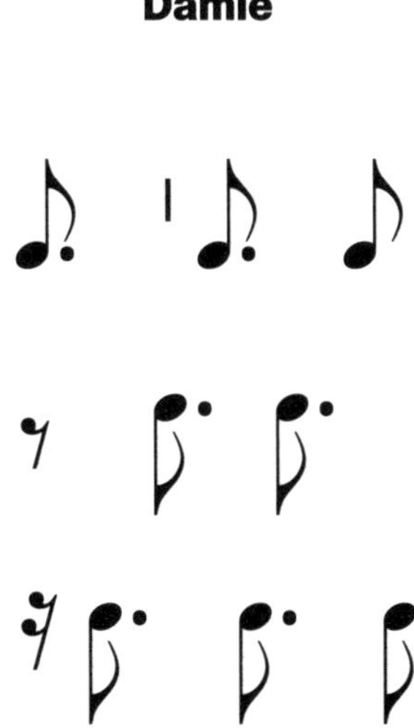

Like the families of *Bèlè* through the operation of the great (*ti*), the extension to the *Gwoka* demonstrates the *Pi Tak* arrangements for finding a balance through the seven rhythms of the *Gwoka*.

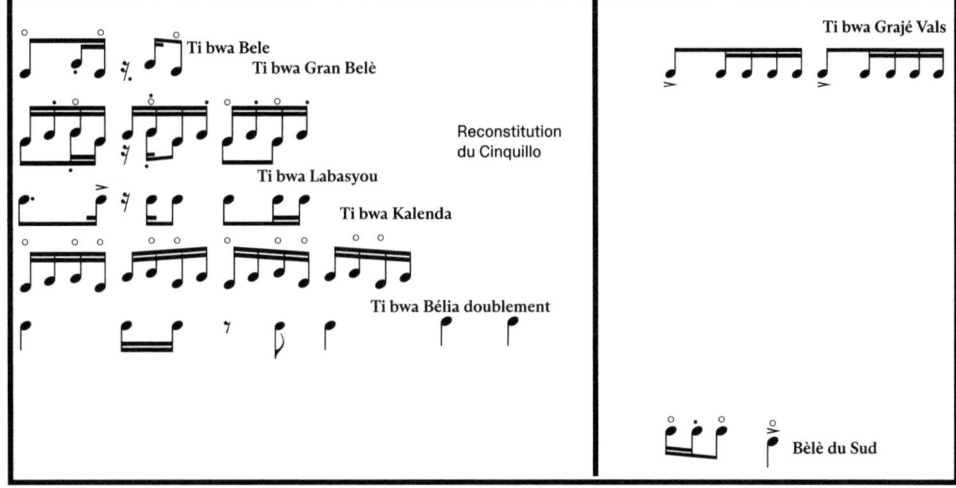

The Harmony of *Tjou pou tèt fouytè / Bèlè*

The revolution through the verb comes from *Blipter*, the world through *Pi Tak*, to combine the gift of *contredon* in inversion with the theft of servile labor. We thus proceed to the inversion of the term work: what was stolen by the creed of inhumanity is exchanged in a circle of reciprocity for an object of sharing in order to re-establish humanity.

The differentiation between the *Bèlè*, a square dance, and the *fouytè*, a labor song, comes from the inverse symmetrical superimpositions of the *ti bwa Bèlè* and the *Yonn a lot* of the drum.

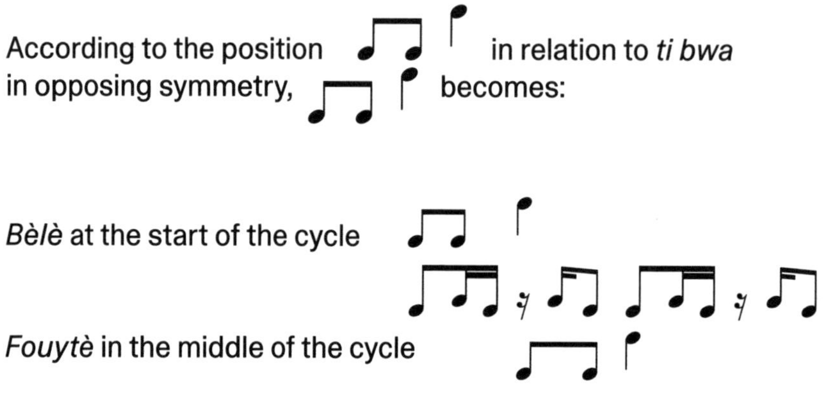

Bwatè / Tanbou: Bèlè / Fouytè
reference cells

What is a flaw in *Bèlè*, i.e. playing the rhythm backwards, is correct and valid in *Fouytè* and we can apply this reasoning in the opposite direction, from *Fouytè*.

This inversion establishes the link between work on the land and celebratory dances, but generally reconciles subsistence and well-being. It corresponds to a symmetry of transformations based on the *Bèlè* and the *Fouytè*, which serve as the basis for the multiplication of combinations by groups of transformations:

Bèlè	☐Dance	☐Energy	☐Celebration	☐*Bèle lè*	☐*Bélya*
Fouytè	☐Labor	☐Food	☐Work	☐Position	☐Society
				(to establish)	

In fact, in the *Bèlè* of Santa Maria, the musical inversion is expressed through mutual help, which is established with the *fouytè*, and the relationship between subsistence and rejoicing, through the *Bèlè*. These two musical practices artistically formalize an objective: to establish who identifies themselves through a *Bèlè*.[13]

Blip and *Pi Tak* are not just sounds. They embody a cultural and philosophical revolution where disorder becomes a source of creation. By reshaping humanity in chaos, as proposed by Léna Blou, these sounds demonstrate that the improbable can generate a profound coherence and universal humanity.[14]

The verb *Blip* orders the formulation of the chaotic outbreak, and the verb *Pi Tak* controls the unpredictability of what happens.

1   Gabriel Entiope, *Nègres, danse et résistance la Caraïbe du XVIIe au XIXe siècle*. Paris: L'Harmattan, 1996, p.52

2   Jean-Baptiste Labat, *Nouveau voyage aux isles de l'Amérique. Tome 2/, Contenant l'histoire naturelle de ces pays, l'origine, les moeurs, la religion & le Gouvernenment des Habitiants anciens & modernes*. La Haye: 1724, p.52.

3   Étienne Jean-Baptiste, *Les musiques de Martinique: une référence à un mode social alternatif*. Fort-de-France: Mizik Label, 2008, p.6.

4   Ibid.

5   Léna Blou, *Le Bigidi, la danse de l'harmonie du désordre: immanence sociale du corps dansant des Antilles et de la Guyane,* PhD Dissertation. Guadeloupe: Anthropology of Dance, Université Antilles-Guyane, 2021, p.28.

6   Étienne Jean-Baptiste, 2008, op. cit., pp.9-10.

7   Ibid., p.18.

8   Ibid.

9   It's worth remembering that the *ti bwa* can be played with both hands.

10   Ibid., p.15.

11   Léna Blou, 2021, op. cit., p.30.

12   Ibid., p.556.

13   A beautiful position.

14   Léna Blou, 2021, op. cit., pp.35-36.

Heitor's Dream

Bruno Pinheiro

On May 13, 1938, the journalist Carlos Cavalcanti published an article in the Rio de Janeiro newspaper *Diário da Noite* in which he presented a set of four canvases produced by the musician and painter Heitor dos Prazeres (1898-1966).[1] The artist was already known to the Rio de Janeiro newspapers as a composer of Carnival songs recorded over the past decade and as a musician in bands of various musical genres. At the time of the article's publication, however, Prazeres' presence in articles about the world of music had diminished, and he had taken up painting as a daily habit.

This radical change in his artistic practices reflected the crossroads the artist had reached. His first wife, Glória dos Prazeres, had recently died. The political anxiety generated by the *coup d'état* perpetrated by Getúlio Vargas in November of the previous year led many intellectuals to look for stable jobs. At this time, the artist began working as a janitor – considered a low-paying, unskilled position – at the Ministry of Education and Health. The dissolution of Black militant organizations by the Estado Novo had stifled many of the commemorative activities marking the fiftieth anniversary of the abolition of formal slavery in Brazil, which had inspired the collaboration between Prazeres and Cavalcanti.[2] Before long, the country would be taken over by a jingoistic discourse that would be consolidated with the creation of the Department of Press and Propaganda in 1939.

Prazeres prepared four canvases for the interview with Cavalcanti. In his article, the journalist highlights the painter's concern with contributing to the production of images that could counteract the negative stereotypes associated with Black people that circulated in his time. In particular, he emphasized the negative images produced about religions of African origin in Brazil, as is suggested by the long debate between the two about the *Macumba* canvas, described in the article. At the same time, Cavalcanti aligns this work with the political projects defended by Prazeres and the current narrative of the history of modern art.[3] The journalist then briefly describes *Jongo*, in which Prazeres contrasts the scene of a Black man being tortured on a farm in colonial Brazil with a group of Black men and women celebrating freely; *Arrebalde*, in which the painter portrays a romantic satire about a couple living in the city's new suburbs; and *Sonho* [Dream], in which he creates a self-portrait immersed in a dreamlike environment.

The four works presented in the article reveal the diversity of Prazeres' work at the beginning of his career as a painter. In the years that followed, his paintings were included in exhibitions of predominantly white modernist artists, held in prestigious spaces throughout Brazil. In this context, a close look at Prazeres' practice of

135

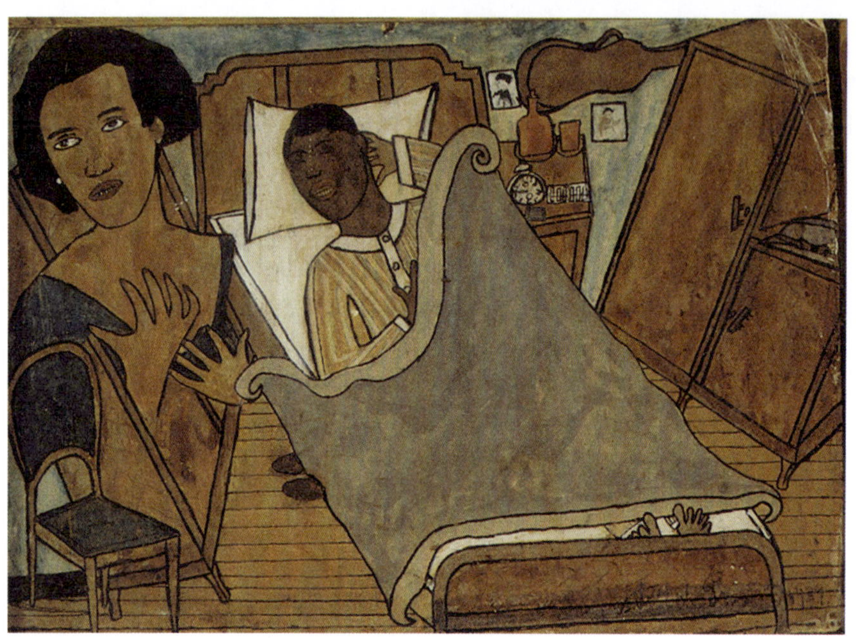

Heitor dos Prazeres
Sonho, 1939
Gouache on cardboard, 19.5 × 27.2 cm
Almeida & Dale Collection
Photo: Sergio Guerini

self-representation in *Sonho* allows us to uncover clues about his practice as a painter in the early years of his career, and his social experience as one of the many Black men who ventured to produce their subjectivities as artists during the 20th century.

In *Sonho*, Prazeres portrays himself in a deep sleep. He is wearing bright yellow striped pajamas under a blanket drawn like a stylized illustration of the surface of the sea. In the composition, the painter is at the center of a spiral perspective that seems to drag the furniture and objects towards itself. This effect is created by the unstable relationship between the parallel, rhythmic lines that form the floor of this enclosed space and the diagonal lines that give volume to the furniture. In this dense environment of objects, the serene face of a woman floats like a vision next to his head.

Like the maritime blanket, the position of each object in the scene seems to suggest relationships that oscillate between the triviality of the painter's everyday life and the construction of a dreamlike and polysemic universe. The hat on the dresser and the guitar on the

136

wall speak of an urban and musical life. The painter's hand reaching for his heart is mirrored in the gesture made by the female figure. At the same time, the correspondence between the shoes coming out from under the bed and her feet slipping through the blanket suggests the thought of a game of correspondence between the objects in the scene. In this way, Prazeres provokes the viewer to immerse themselves in the details of the image.

Over the two decades that followed, Prazeres made a number of self-portraits. In the vast majority of them, the portrayal of himself emerges as an act of affirmation of his own individuality, as Renata Bittencourt notes in her analysis of the self-portrait *O artista* [The Artist] (1959).[4] In the case of this particular canvas, the writer draws attention to certain aspects of Prazeres' subjectivity suggested by the painting – such as the recognition of his own maturity, and the relationship between his poetics and the visual forms present in spaces of Umbanda worship – a religion practiced by the painter. On the other hand, the considerable number of self-portraits in which Prazeres creates images of himself while practicing his craft was also a response to the ongoing development of a professional identity as an artist.

The sense of mistrust generated by the post-abolition Brazilian elite toward Black professionals made the self-portrait a practice of professional self-affirmation throughout the 20th century. This is what Kleber Amancio observes in his analysis of three self-portraits produced by Arthur Timóteo da Costa (1882-1922) during the first two decades of the 20th century. During this period, the painter, who was also Black, had access to prestigious educational institutions between his hometown of Rio de Janeiro and Paris.[5]

In these cases, self-representation creates projections of oneself that denote the dignity and stability present in the culture of respectability shared by Black men who sought out experiences of entering the world of professional work throughout the 20th century. In the case of Prazeres' 1938 canvas, its originality lies in the exercise of representing projections of himself that inhabit the dreamlike space of thought inhabited by vagueness, in which his social and professional desires can collide with his vulnerabilities. A similar practice can be seen decades later in the paintings, engravings, and drawings of Sidney Amaral (1973–2017), in which his immersion in the symbols of his own unconscious allowed him to create a poetics steeped in critical projections of himself.

Among the many self-portraits Amaral made over the years, *Enigma entre eu e tu* [Enigma between Me and You] reveals profound questions about the painter's daily work.[6] In the painting, the painter portrays himself staring at a figure that seems to be made up of the dismantled parts of a mannequin. Although the figure has a shape associated with the female body in clothing stores, its face resembles that of the painter himself. The arrangement of the objects seems to tell a story. The figure appears to have been taken from an open trunk at the bottom of the composition and placed on a drawing board. The artist is leaning on the chair that forms the workspace, facing his own work, which, like a riddle, comes to life in the daily struggle of work.

The composition of Amaral's work is easily identifiable with Jean-Auguste Dominique Ingres' *Oedipus and the Sphinx* (1808). Amaral's self-portrait as Oedipus has a line similar to Ingres', which continuously outlines his body arched towards the Sphinx from his feet to the top of his head. On the Frenchman's canvas, Oedipus subtly points at himself and the Sphinx, while unraveling his riddle: What has four legs in the morning, two legs at noon and three legs at dusk? The answer would be 'man' (in the supposedly universal sense produced by the Enlightenment) in his different stages of life.[7] Or perhaps Amaral's Oedipus would be the Black man, faced with his own vulnerabilities as he recognizes himself trying to assemble the parts of his own riddle without being devoured.

Prazeres' work at the moment of his transformation into a painter, and Amaral's work as he faced the daily grind, emerge from profoundly different contexts. However, their works share the common experience of having been produced by Black men who, in their own way, were attentive to the production of their own subjectivity as artists. A craft they practiced without ignoring the meanings of their images and the clashes produced by the social relations in which they lived.

1   Carlos Cavalcanti and Heitor dos Prazeres, "O brando gesto da princesa..." *Diário da Noite*, Rio de Janeiro, n.3.236, p.2, May, 1938.

2   On some experiences of silencing the memory of abolition that year, see: Paulina L. Alberto, *Termos da Inclusão: intelectuais negros brasileiros no século XX*. Campinas: Editora da Unicamp, 2017.

3   I analyze the dialog about this painting in more detail in Bruno Pinheiro, "Moenda de Heitor dos Prazeres, medalha de prata na I Bienal do Museu de Arte Moderna de São Paulo," *Revista de História da Arte e da Cultura*, v.2, n.2, 2021.

4   Renata Bittencourt, "Sou eu que dou as regras: a autorrepresentação de Heitor dos Prazeres," *Revista ARS*, v.20, n.45, Aug. 2022.

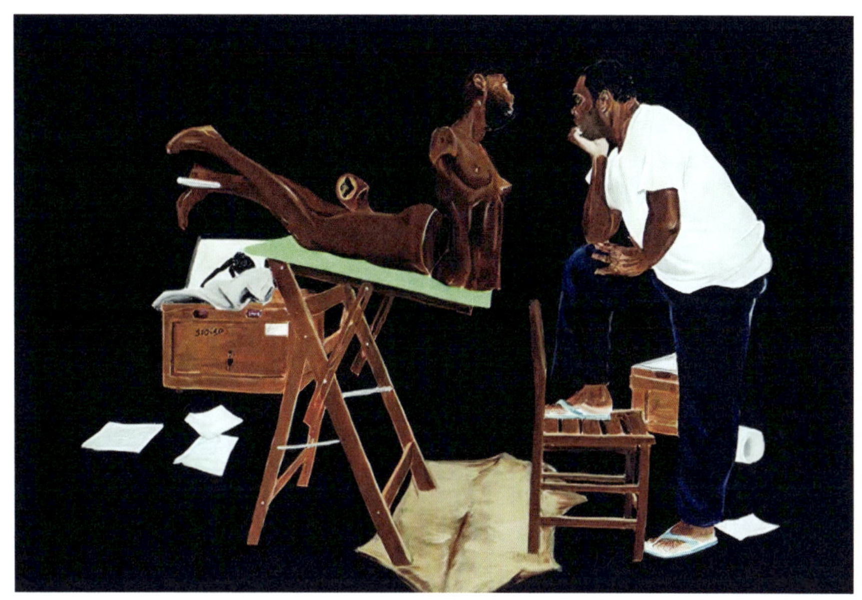

Sidney Amaral
Enigma entre eu e tu, 2014
Oil on canvas, 140 × 210 cm,
Sesc Art Collection

5   Kleber A. O. Amancio, "Os autorretratos de Arthur Timotheo da Costa, um ensaio sobre a autorrepresentação," in Martha Abreu et al. (eds.), *Histórias do pós-abolição no mundo atlântico: identidades e projetos políticos*, v.1. Niterói: Editora da UFF, 2013.

6   Claudinei Roberto da Silva presented this work in the context of Sidney Amaral's self-portraits in Claudinei Roberto da Silva, *Viver até o fim que me cabe! Sidney Amaral: uma aproximação*. Jundiaí: SESC-SP, 2021.

7   On the critique of the Enlightenment subject, see: Denise Ferreira da Silva, *A dívida impagável*. São Paulo: Oficina de Imaginação Política and Living Commons, 2019.

Following the Trail of Choreographic Escapes: An Archipelagic Writing in Dance

Lazaro Benitez

Conference held during *Invocation #2* on December 7, 2024.

What fundamental elements can we extract from choreographic writing and performance in the insular Caribbean? Does this condition produce one or more aesthetics? To what extent do contemporary dance and performance feed into these questions?

I think there's something unique about this choreography. We might think that an island, due to its geographical condition, is forced into a form of isolation; however, as Édouard Glissant reminds us, "islands are not isolated. They are chained. They didn't make history, but they lived it, and that's how they often correct it."[1]

In this text, I propose a kind of journey through a few figures in contemporary Caribbean dance and their works. This research is located in the territories of Cuba, Haiti, the Dominican Republic, Guadeloupe, and Martinique.

141

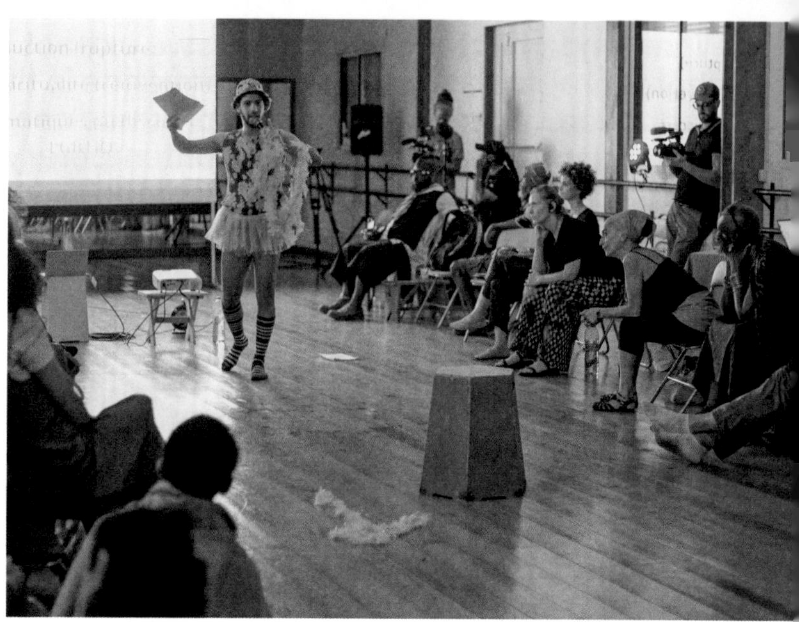

All photos: © Philippe Hurgon /
Fundação Bienal de São Paulo

Before a Poetics of the Diverse

Since the mid-20th century, the Caribbean has often been defined in para-doxical terms. Whether we're talking about a "sea that diffracts" (Édouard Glissant), an "island that repeats itself" (Antonio Benítez Rojo) or a "subma-rine unity" (Edward Kamau Brathwaite), the insularity that characterizes the Caribbean region comes into tension with an abstract unity that tran-scends the different borders – concrete or symbolic – that divide it into disparate fragments.

The first clue to approaching the problem that I would like to share with you is therefore that of the *border*. How does one think about the border of an island? What is this border?

Writers and artists regularly explore this ambivalence, making the notion of the border a central issue in the representation and definition of the Caribbean islands. At once an intrinsic feature of the Caribbean territory and an indelible mark of the colonial period, the border is also constantly reconfigured, becoming an essential site of debate about a possible identity for the Caribbean space. How do the works reaf-firm – or otherwise – this border space?

142

Geographical borders are also perceived by Caribbean artists as signs of *historical rupture*. The Atlantic trade and slavery gave the Atlantic Ocean a border-like dimension which separated the newcomers to the Caribbean islands from their African origins. These forced displacements led to a memorial fragmentation that continued in subsequent diasporas. According to Derek Walcott: "The Caribbean artist can be seen as one who brings together the fragmentary memories of various cultures, overcoming the historical boundaries that separate Caribbean societies from their lost origins in order to conceive a common history."
Derek Walcott's definition highlights the historical complexity of our territory. Our memory is neither unidirectional nor exact. It is diverse, made up of multiple sources: first the tools and narratives of the colonizers, then our own tools. This memory, fragmented like the islands in its composition, brings us back to the notion of the archipelago.

The reflection on the overcoming of historical borders is part of a wider cultural debate, which has been constantly evolving since the mid-20th century. Artists regularly recall that the Caribbean islands, as we conceive them today, *"were born in colonization"* (Patrick Chamoiseau). Their work tends to reconfigure the multiple borders drawn since modern times into sites conducive to the development of an open and plural Caribbean identity.

Based on the observation of linguistic miscegenation operated since the European conquest, which gave rise to Creole, mutant, and varied languages, they envision a Caribbean culture that is intrinsically *"border-like,"* marked by its hybridity. *"Antilleanity,"* a concept of rhizomatic Caribbean identity developed by Édouard Glissant in the 1960s, found an extension in the notion of *"creolity"* used by Patrick Chamoiseau and Raphaël Confiant in the 1980s. Although it has been the subject of much debate, this concept has paved the way for new approaches to creolization.

If we consider the border as the *"open wound"* defined by Gloria Anzaldúa in *Borderlands: La Frontera/La Nueva Mestiza*, it seems that for such a wound to exist, two parts must be placed in tension: the skin opens and, depending on the angle at which one is placed, one part becomes more visible than the other. Thus, there is *the skin, the emptiness of the wound, and then the skin again*. This separation into fragments, although made of the same material, creates a space of alterity that we could call *"the other part."* It is precisely from this notion that I conceive of the *margin*: the other part of the injury, this other side of the physical border exposed to alterity. Like a rock that faces the incessant attacks of the waves, the margin suffers the direct impact of alterity, in permanence.

143 Caribbean societies are deeply structured around various types of migratory movements: rural exodus, inter-Caribbean migrations or even the broader diasporic phenomena linked to the colonial and contemporary eras. These dynamics imply a constant reterritorialization of our relationship with the space we inhabit. These phenomena force us to construct ourselves as fragmented beings, like a *collage*. In the words of Cuban anthropologist Fernando Ortiz, "a cultural *ajiaco*," bringing together disparate elements to make up an identity that is both fluid and complex.

The Margin as Poetic Strategy

What interests me here is talking to you about the work of different artists from this insular area of the Caribbean islands, who have created a space of resistance and a place to live. This invitation implies an epistemological shift to explore practices that reappropriate the margin as a place of poetic and aesthetic production: *the "aesthetics of the margin."*

As such, we are witnessing an act of dignification, not only of the margin as a place of expression for the artists we are going to refer to, but also of other forms of margins. The notion of the *margin* can be revealed more clearly depending on the context in which it is approached. We come to this space of the margin not only because it is attributed to us, but also out of recognition: we understand that we don't fully belong elsewhere and therefore decide to live in and from this margin. An aesthetic of the margin, firstly, questions the universal way of inhabiting our current world and also restores the power of practices that are marginalized by the dominant system.

The Artists in Question

In pursuing this reflection on an aesthetic of the margin, three axes that emerge from the works of the artists in this study seem to me to be fundamental in deconstructing this category. These axes are: the reinvention of the ritual as an open and rhizomatic hybrid form; the translation and reappropriation of traditional Caribbean dances; and the most recent updating and resituation of LGBTQIA+ discourses and themes stemming from an insular context.

Johan Mijail

Born in Santo Domingo, 1990, is a journalist, writer, and performer. His work explores the construction of transfeminist and decolonial imaginaries, with a Caribbean perspective that he calls *"transvestite epistemologies of a Black Caribbean body."*

In *Amor vegetal* [Plant Love], Johan Mijail extends his reflection as an author and performer to Nature, creating an invisible link with the Cuban-American artist Ana Mendieta and her work *Flores en el cuerpo* [Flowers on Body], from the *Siluetas* [Silhouettes] series. Johan Mijail creates a normative or cisgender rupture in the theme of the principle of life, creation and fertilization. He uses his anus as the principle of life, as a generator of new forms of creation. In his performance, the artist enters the space, undresses, washes his intimate parts with a beer can – a gesture that invites us to reflect on the rituality of the act, its precision and how the sense of cleanliness and purity becomes a determining element in sexual-affective interactions. This is especially true in the case of homosexual men, where an elaborate ritual of preparation, especially for those who play the passive role, often precedes the act.

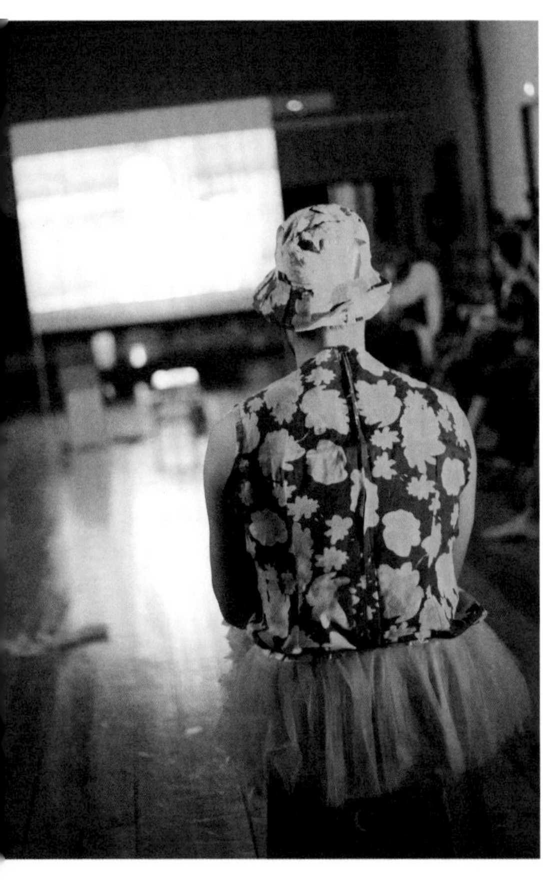

In this regard, it recalls Paul B. Preciado: "Historically, the anus has been considered an abject organ, never clean enough, never silent enough. It is not and cannot be politically correct. The anus does not produce, or more precisely, it only produces waste."[2]

Johan Mijail remarks that "plant love means suffering a loss in the sense of reproductive sexuality, preferring to devote time to investigating how terrestrial and marine plants collaborate with each other, so as not to think about the institution of the couple. Plant love is a technology of the self that considers waste as a possible space. All of this with the idea of producing an escape, a modification or an interruption in the flow of history."

Annabel Guérédrat

Born in 1974 in Noumea, New Caledonia, she lives and works in Martinique. A choreographer, dancer, performer, researcher and *"bruja,"* she is also a practitioner of body-mind centering, a somatic practice that allows her to write (eco/afro) feminist, organic performances, where the intimate and the political are increasingly linked. Annabel Guérédrat's three main performances, inspired by modern figures of witches, are: *A Freak Show for S, Hysteria* (2010) and *I'm a Bruja* (2018).

I'm a Bruja is an act that aims to reinvent our rituals, to rebuild our affective ties with the witches, goddesses and spirits that surround our Caribbean cosmovision. In a circular space, the choreographer and performer summons the presence of various witches, artists, authors, poets, philosophers, and singers, such as Audre Lorde, bell hooks, Elsa Dorlin, Nina Hagen, Ana Mendieta, and Princess Nokia.

In *I'm a Bruja*, the scenography, also stripped down, is essentially organized around a circle drawn on the floor, which constitutes the central axis of the performance, similar to a margin and, at the same time, works on the notion of margin. The circle is circumscribed by lit candles whose light is reinforced by neon lights placed on the floor along its internal perimeter.

This fixed double luminosity seems to perform a double function: it delimits the space from the outside thanks to the layout of the candles, and the neon lights work on the interior luminosity of the circle while reflecting their light on the body of the performer sitting in its center. This installation highlights feminine beauty in its natural state. A mixed-race woman with loose hair and silky curls is completely naked. Standing there, her gestures are executed with a slight slowness, with a soft sensuality. In this mystical environment with soft lighting, the viewer is watching an intimate scene that could represent the daily ablutions of a woman who exudes an animal, almost savage sensuality. This installation scene, within a precise perimeter, is the setting for the witch character constructed by Annabel Guérédrat.

Annabel creates her own codes using almost constant nudity on stage. Her belly, vulva and pubis are shown several times during a movement, a gesture. In the first figure, an animal and animist witch, she gets on all fours and, leaning on her hands, puts her head on the ground, her pelvis raised, stretches out a leg, letting you guess her vulva is wide open, her labia open. She shows her vulva two or three times, including the inside, as if showing the singular beauty of the female sex between demonstrating and claiming the specificity of this part of the body.

In Conclusion

Through their works, these artists speak of the fissures generated by our hegemonic system and the implications that these fissures trigger in order to offer space to other bodies. To enter the fissure like a bacterium, to generate the disease to regenerate another skin.

To save the pains of colonial history to heal them, to repair them through a symbolic act that is the theatrical act. They defend, through their bodies, the possibility of creating their right to belong to a territory, through its forms, expanding the possibility of reinventing and regenerating it. They inaugurate a language with the rubble, the silences, the voids left by colonial history. They feed the Caribbean territory with these corporealities and narratives that have been and continue to be very controversial. They also feed the border because, as Gloria Anzaldúa says: *Los atravesados*[3] live there: the weirdos, the perverts, the queers, the troublemakers, the bastards, the mulattos, the mestizos, and the living dead; in short, everyone who has already crossed over to the other side of the norm. They construct the Caribbean space as a laboratory of possibilities.

1   Édouard Glissant. *Les Discours antillais*. Paris: Folio, 1997, p.87.
2   Paul B. Preciado, *Manifiesto contra-sexual*. Madrid: Opera Prima, 2002.
3   A person who no longer wishes to follow the flow imposed by their context and who opposes it, thus breaking the course of history.

Educational Activities

The practices in the educational publication for the 36th Bienal de São Paulo are developed by the Fundação Bienal de São Paulo with the aim of bringing the world of contemporary art closer to different pedagogical contexts, promoting a type of education that recognizes subjectivity and the plurality of experiences, understanding those who take part as protagonists in these processes. It was built with teachers from São Paulo's public school system[1] and is in line with the Brazilian National Common Core Curriculum (BNCC) guidelines.

Designed as scripts for Creative Laboratories, they are arranged into three meetings that can be adapted and incorporated according to the needs and possibilities of each context, with the aim of encouraging the construction of integrated knowledge, the expression of ideas, feelings, and reflections on social and cultural issues. Here, the sequence of meetings is based on the concepts of teacher and choreographer Léna Blou, who in her research reflects on *Bigidi* as a Caribbean expression of the body and culture. "Danced Movements" articulates dance as a tool for experimentation and collaboration based on the circularity and integration of individual and collective repertoires. In "Soundscapes," we invite you to reflect on the artist Emeka Ogboh, extrapolating the visual dimension of landscapes in the process of investigating the meanings and histories of the spaces we inhabit through sounds.

149

Danced Movements

In dialogue with the contents of *Invocation #2*, the "Danced Movements" activity proposes a series of meetings with the aim of experimenting with dance through games, improvisation, and the sharing of individual and collective repertoires.

OBJECTIVE:

→ Relating contemporary art to everyday life
→ Experimenting with different forms of orientation in space and rhythms of movement
→ Improvising and creating movements individually and collectively
→ Establishing collaborative creative relationships between people through the materialities of movement that emerge

REQUIRED MATERIALS:

→ Balloons
→ Writing materials (felt pens)
→ Audio speaker

DEVELOPMENT:

In educational spaces where art plays a role in the fruition of knowledge, dance creation processes manifest themselves in different ways, with specific vocabularies depending on the location, style/modality, and dance proposals. One example is the funk *Passinho*, a dance created by young people living in *favelas* in Brazil, which has variations in movement and nomenclature depending on the region of the country. *Passinho Malado* from Belo Horizonte (MG) and *Passinho dos Maloka* from Recife (PE) are some of the variations that denote specific movement compositions.

This activity is not intended to instruct on how to perform a particular style of dance, but rather to sensitize the body in order to provoke expressiveness, creativity, and the exchange of experiences inherent in the activity between participants from each location. Meetings can be held in large, open spaces with no furniture, such as a sports court or schoolyard.

MEETING 1 – MOVING AROUND

In this meeting, people will be invited to experiment with body movements through games that include displacement, spatial directions, weight, flow, and time.

Arrange the class in a circle and start the meeting with a body warm-up. One suggestion is to move the whole body, drawing large shapes in space, alternating with small gestures that call for the use of different joints. After warming up, hand out a balloon to each participant and play the following game:

→ Invite them to blow up the balloons slowly and quickly, experimenting with the different sensations: changes in breathing and body movements

→ After experimenting with the different intensities of breathing, help them tie knots in the filled balloons

→ Invite the class to play with the balloons by throwing them upwards. Experiment with different parts of the body by not letting the balloons fall to the ground

→ Put on some music to accompany the action and experiment with different forms of movement, such as slow, moderate, and fast

→ At the end of the game, invite participants to write a word on the balloon that refers to their experience, using a marker pen

151

Talk about the bodily sensations you got from playing the game. Forming a circle, use the words written on the balloons to share your impressions of the meeting.

MEETING 2 – IMPROVISATION GAME

This meeting will work on elements of improvisation and creation through a game that combines aspects of movement, allowing for experimentation with, and experience of, dance.

Start the meeting with a body warm-up. Invite people to walk around the space at different speeds: slow, moderate, and fast. During the walks, suggest sudden pauses. Next, try walking/moving on different spatial levels: low, medium, and high. Finally, combine the different times and spatial levels. After the warm-up, suggest the following improvisation game: a proposal to activate the dancing body by drawing cards with different instructions which generate combinations for exploring movement creatively:

→ **Access the improvisation game cards (QR Code) and print them out, or make the cards using available materials, considering the following:**

TIME cards: three cards printed double-sided
    front TIME – back SLOW
    front TIME – back MODERATE
    front TIME – back FAST

SPACE LEVEL cards: three cards printed double-sided
    front SPACE LEVEL – back LOW
    front SPACE LEVEL – back MEDIUM
    front SPACE LEVEL – back HIGH

MOVEMENT cards: three cards printed double-sided
    front MOVEMENT – back FRAGMENTED
    front MOVEMENT – back ARTICULATED /
    DISARTICULATED
    front MOVEMENT – back SYMMETRICAL / ASYMMETRICAL

→   **Present the improvisation game cards: TIME (slow, moderate, fast) /
    SPACE LEVELS (low, closer to the ground; medium, sitting position or
    equivalent; high, standing) / MOVEMENT (fragmented, articulated/
    disarticulated, symmetrical/asymmetrical)**
→   **Invite the group to draw one card from each instruction: TIME –
    SPACE LEVELS – MOVEMENT**
→   **Ask people to combine the instructions drawn. For example: TIME
    card: slow + SPACE LEVELS card: high + MOVEMENT card:
    symmetrical/asymmetrical**
→   **Use music to accompany the movement improvisations inspired by
    the drawn instructions**
→   **Determine the time it takes to improvise the movements for each
    round of card combinations**

Forming a circle, talk about how the improvisation game went. Make space
for everyone to share their impressions. Here are some suggested questions
for the conversation:

> *What was it like performing the improvisation game?*
> *What movement types do you have the strongest affinity for?*
> *Do you feel like you're dancing with this proposal?*

Finally, instruct the class to bring songs to the next meeting that are reminiscent of the dances they like to practise, with the aim of creating a dance
experience based on the choices they have brought in.

Game Cards

MEETING 3 – DANCES WE LIKE

In order to revisit the routes taken and prepare for the next proposal, start the meeting with a body warm-up, using elements from previous meetings, such as movement with the balloon or the improvisation game.

After the warm-up, organize the class for the presentations of the *Dances We Like*, based on the pre-selected songs. The dances can be presented individually or in groups, inspired by the form of soirees or dance battles, but without the purpose of it being a competition. Provide a meeting for the exchange of artistic expression, with circularity and improvisation as its essence.

At the end of the presentations, provide space for everyone to share their impressions. Here are some suggested questions for the conversation:

What was it like performing the dances we like?
What were the discoveries and difficulties?
What are the relationships between the dances presented?

Invite the class to continue researching new dances with the aim of broadening their artistic repertoires.

SUGGESTIONS FOR FURTHER WORK:

Organize a dance festival at the venue with the involvement of the community.

154

Soundscapes

This series of meetings seeks to get closer to the sound projects running through the 36th Bienal de São Paulo, based on the research and creation of soundscapes in dialogue with the work of artists such as Emeka Ogboh.

OBJECTIVE

→ Relating contemporary art and everyday life
→ Creating soundscapes
→ Discussing the relationship between cultural landscapes and soundscapes
→ Experimenting with different forms of artistic expression

REQUIRED MATERIALS

→ Materials that can make sounds (everyday objects)
→ Musical instruments

DEVELOPMENT:

When talking about landscape, there are common associations with images of nature with little or no human interference. However, according to geography, the notion of landscape is not limited to natural landscapes. Large cities and agricultural plantations in rural areas are examples of human intervention in space and are therefore called cultural landscapes. It is interesting to note that both types of landscapes are not comprehended by sight alone and can be experienced through various sensory stimuli.

Is it possible to grasp a landscape through hearing? How do the sounds of the spaces we live in impact our lives? For decades, these questions have motivated researchers from various fields and artists from different disciplines. In this activity we seek to discuss and create soundscapes.

MEETING 1 – GETTING TO KNOW SOUNDSCAPES

In the first meeting with the class, we recommend perception exercises that can be done outdoors or at a location that has a special meaning for the group. The activity is intended to enable each participant to map the sounds of the environment and thus perceive the soundscape of the space in which the action takes place. At this point, we suggest a dynamic inspired by some of Viola Spolin's[2] *Teather Games*:

→ Once the group is assembled, invite people to remain silent with their eyes closed for a certain amount of time
→ Next, tell them to concentrate on their heartbeats, then the closest sounds, and then the more distant sounds
→ These steps can be repeated and the order changed

Next, we recommend that each participant write down the sounds heard in the environment during the exercise and share them with the group. At this point, it's important to observe the ways in which people name common elements (Do they recognize where it comes from? What or who produced it?) and encourage the group to interpret the soundscape (What does it sound like? What information does it provide about the territory?).

This activity can also serve as an introduction to a discussion on the concept of the soundscape and the work of sound artist Emeka Ogboh.[3]

157

Born in Enugu, Nigeria, Ogboh now lives in Berlin and says that when he feels homesick, he listens to recordings of the street sounds of Lagos, a city known for being one of the noisiest on the African continent. But the artist seems to disagree with this statement, since, as he sees it, the city doesn't produce only noise, but a type of composition.

→   **Scan the QR Code to access "Danfo Melow," a track from the album _Beyond The Yellow Haze_ by Emeka Ogboh**

From this kind of prompt, you could ask the class:
If the sounds of the city in which the group lives were a composition, what kind of music would it be? Has it always been like this? What could it be like?

At the end of the meeting, the mediator can ask each participant to do the same exercise at home, recording the sounds of the place where they live at a certain time of day. This can be done in the form of notes in a notebook or a recording of the local soundscape.

"Danfo Melow"
by Emeka Ogboh

MEETING 2 – SHARING SOUNDSCAPES

The second meeting can begin with a circle in which each participant shares their collection of sounds with the group. We suggest a few topics for this exchange:

Questions for describing each sound individually:
- → **What is the timbre of this sound like?**
- → **Do you know where it came from?**
- → **Do you know who or what produced this sound?**

Questions for the description of the soundscape:
- → **Is there any music playing in this soundscape? Do you know the music being played?**
- → **Are there birds or other animals in this soundscape? Do you recognize the species?**

After the exchange, you can propose a moment of analysis of the common elements of the soundscapes. Again, it's important to observe how each participant names the sounds. From this point, a vocabulary can be created about what the group has heard. All of this can be compared with the soundscape of the environment in which the activity is taking place. A discussion can also be held about the difference in the sounds of places in dialogue with broader questions about territories.

We recommend that the mediator record and organize the collective's ideas and the vocabulary developed by the group for the next meeting.

159

MEETING 3 – CREATING SOUNDSCAPES

We recommend that the last meeting be geared towards a collective production of soundscapes, based on the material produced in the second meeting:

→ Based on the ideas and vocabulary developed in Meeting 2, research and choose materials and musical instruments that can represent the sounds of the soundscapes
→ With the group present, show them the materials, instruments, and elements of the soundscapes evoked in the previous meeting
→ Ask the people in the group to choose the sounds from the soundscape and their respective objects/instruments
→ "Conduct" the group by representing the soundscape (this action can be done by the mediator or alternated between the people in the group)
→ After the performance, you can also create other soundscapes by observing different natural or cultural landscapes
→ End with a discussion about the experience

SUGGESTIONS FOR FURTHER WORK:

Put on a collective performance based on recreating the soundscapes, where each participant in the group represents its elements with body movements.

This series of meetings can also inspire the creation of a sound/music improvisation session using everyday objects.

1   We would like to thank Bel Borges, Durval Mantovaninni, Gustavo Viana, Kaya Fernanda Vallim Braga Martins, Maria da Conceição Ferreira da Silva, Pamela Regina, and Rodrigo Pignatari for the rich exchanges that took place on October 26 and November 9, 2024.

2   Viola Spolin was born in Chicago, United States, in 1906. She studied Philosophy and Literature at the University of Chicago and was an actress, theater director, and educator. She is known for the creation of "theater games," combining playful, and scenic activities, mainly based on the principles of Bertolt Brecht and Stanislavski.

3   Emeka Ogboh was born in Nigeria in 1977 and currently lives in Berlin. The artist investigates urban transformations based on a multi-sensory geography, such as musical perception, noise, the smell of the streets, and local cuisine. His creations provide access to both public and private histories and memories. He has participated in several exhibitions, including documenta 14 and the 56th Venice Biennale.

About
the Authors

Alya Sebti is a contemporary art curator and director of the ifa-Galerie (Institut für Auslandsbeziehungen) in Berlin, where she initiated the research and exhibition platform *Untie to Tie – On Colonial Legacies in Contemporary Societies*. She was co-curator of the European biennial Manifesta in Marseille (2020), guest curator of the Dakar Biennale (2018), and artistic director of the Marrakech Biennale (2014). She has led curatorial research through mentorship programs at the ZK/U artist residency (Berlin) and at MACAAL (Marrakech).

Anaïs Verspan is a visual artist. She began her career in fashion design, opening the Afro Excentrik showroom after three years of study at the Regional Institute of Visual Arts in Martinique. Her works have already been exhibited in Senegal, Germany, Monaco, and Portugal. Her visual world balances abstraction and figuration, past and present, creating pieces that explore cultural duality and individual experiences.

Anna Roberta Goetz is a curator and writer. She has worked at the Marta Herford Museum and the MMK Museum für Moderne Kunst Frankfurt. She was assistant curator and project manager of the German Pavilion at the 55th Venice Biennale (2013). She has organized major solo and group exhibitions in various countries and has taught at several international art academies, including the Zurich University of the Arts and the Städelschule in Frankfurt. Her publications include *Rodney McMillian: The Land: Not Without a Politic*, co-edited with Kathleen Rahn (2024), and *Cinthia Marcelle – By Means of Doubt*, co-edited with Isabella Rjeille (2023).

163

Bonaventure Soh Bejeng Ndikung is a curator, author, and biotechnologist, currently serving as the director and chief curator of the Haus der Kulturen der Welt (HKW) in Berlin. He is the founder and former artistic director of SAVVY Contemporary in Berlin, as well as the artistic director of sonsbeek20→24 (Arnhem). He is a professor and head of faculty in the Master's program in Spatial Strategies at the weißensee academy of art berlin. His published works include, among others, *The Delusions of Care* (2021), *An Ongoing-Offcoming Tale: Ruminations on Art, Culture, Politics and Us/Others* (2022), and *Pidginization as Curatorial Method* (2023).

Bruno Pinheiro is an art historian, curator, and educator. He holds a PhD in History from Unicamp and is currently a postdoctoral fellow at the Leonard A. Lauder Research Center for Modern Art at the Metropolitan Museum of Art, where he is conducting research on Black modernist artists from Latin America and the Caribbean. He has research and teaching on the history of art and visual culture of the African diaspora in the Americas.

Dory Sélèsprika is a poet and slammer. Her style is influenced by *Gwoka* music, Senjan, and urban cultures. *Tan* is her first poetry collection. Since 2006, she has been collaborating on stage performances, festivals, and literary and recording projects with artists such as Dominik Coco, Jil Pietrus, Didier Juste, Fanm Ki Ka, Laurence Hamlet, Bwakoré, Akiyo.

Edinho Santos holds a degree in pedagogy and works as an educator at Itaú Cultural. He has experience as an educator in museums such as Afro Brasil, MAM-SP, and the Museu do Futebol. In 2017, he won 3rd place in Slam SP. He worked on the film *O matador* (2017). He is an activist in the deaf Black movement and is a producer and slammer at the Slam de Surdes.

Étienne Jean-Baptiste is a trombonist, pianist, composer, and conductor in modern and contemporary *Bèlè* musical experiments, as well as a researcher. He combines anthropology and musical practice in his investigations of *Bèlè*. A PhD graduate from the École des Hautes Études en Sciences Sociales, he is a pioneer in the education of Caribbean arts and cultural practices. He is a member of the Archives, Ethnographic Documents, Caribbean America (ADECAm) at the Université des Antilles.

Geordy Zodidat Alexis is a multi-disciplinary artist. He works with drawing, performance, installation, and writing to explore collective memory and cultural identity. Gratuated of the École Supérieure des Beaux-Arts Montpellier, his work addresses themes such as coexistence and the impact of multiple cultural heritages–Caribbean, African, and European.

Keyna Eleison is a curator, researcher, and educator in art and culture. Eleison coordinated all public institutions from the Rio de Janeiro Municipal Department of Culture and taught at the Escola de Artes Visuais do Parque Lage, where she was also a teaching coordinator. She was the curator of the 10th Bienal Internacional de SIART in Bolivia (2018), the curator of the 1st Bienal das Amazônias (2023), the artistic director of the MAM Rio (2020-2023) and director of research and content at the Bienal das Amazônias.

Lazaro Benitez is a dance researcher and choreographer. He explores the boundaries between dance and performance, addressing themes such as borders, gender, and artistic activism. He holds a master's degree from the Université Paris 8, is the founder of the De la memoria fragmentada laboratory, and a contributor to specialized journals. His work maps contemporary dance in the Caribbean, promoting workshops and lectures that connect society and choreography.

Léna Blou is an anthropologist, dancer, choreographer, and educator. She is a pioneer of the *Bigidi*'art technique. Inspired by the *léwòz* dance, this practice explores the body in imbalance as a form of self-determination. Creator of the contemporary pedagogical method Techni'ka, based on *Gwoka* rhythms and dances, she founded the Center for Dance and Choreography Studies, the Trilogie Léna Blou Company, and the Larel Bigidi'Art. Her work connects artistic practice, research, and education, exploring disorder and adaptability as forms of creative resistance in times of social, political, and environmental precarity.

Lidia Lisbôa's practice encompasses sculpture, crochet, performances, and drawings. Her research explores biographies, landscapes, the body, and memory through materials that capture the artist's gesture. Lisbôa's most recent solo exhibition took place at the Museu de Arte do Rio (2024). She has participated in group shows at Museo Madre (Naples), Palais des Nations (Geneva, Switzerland), and, in São Paulo, at Museu AfroBrasil, Instituto Tomie Ohtake, and Museu de Arte Moderna de São Paulo. The artist was also part of the 13th Mercosul Biennial (Porto Alegre).

Lisbôa's works are in the collections of the Institute for Studies on Latin American Art and El Museo del Barrio (New York), Pinacoteca do Estado de São Paulo, and Sesc São Paulo.

Michelle Mycoo is a professor and researcher. Her work focuses on strengthening the interface between science, politics, and practice, aligning the optimal use of land, infrastructure provision, and environmental management, with the goal of supporting sustainable human settlements. Among her academic contributions are international publications on Caribbean case studies related to urban and regional planning.

Olivier Marboeuf is a writer, storyteller and curator. Since 2004 he has founded and directed the independent art center Espace Khiasma (Les Lilas), on the outskirts of Paris. At Khiasma, he has developed a program addressing minority representations through exhibitions, screenings, debates, performances and collaborative projects throughout northeast Paris. Since 2017, Khiasma has merged with an experimental platform, exploring ways to create a place collectively and developing an online radio tool, R22 Tout-Monde. Interested in different ways of transmitting knowledge, Olivier Marboeuf's proposals are rooted in conversational practices and speculative narratives, attempting to create ephemeral situations of culture.

Santiago Quintana is a software engineer, musician, movement artist, and performer who works in an interdisciplinary way. Among his works is the electroacoustic performance *O Death* (2023).

168

Bienal Archive

Leno Veras – *manager*
Antonio Paulo Carretta – *coordinator*
Marcele Souto Yakabi – *coordinator*
Ana Helena Grizotto Custódio
Anna Beatriz Corrêa Bortoletto
Daniel Malva Ribeiro
Gislene Sales
Gustavo Paes
Kleber Costa Timoteo
Raquel Coelho Moliterno
Thais Ferreira Dias
Alex Reimann – *intern*
Deisy Yumi – *intern*
Eloisa Elena – *intern*
Fabio Silva – *intern*
Juliana Knobel – *intern*
Maíra Alves – *intern*
Ricardo Menezes – *intern*
Walter Rocha – *intern*

Financial and Administrative

Finances

Amarildo Firmino Gomes – *manager*
Edson Pereira de Carvalho – *coordinator*
Fábio Kato
Silvia Andrade Simões Branco

Human Resources

Andréa Moreira – *human resources coordinator*
Higor Tocchio – *payroll and personnel department coordinator*
Matheus Andrade Sartori
Patricia Fernandes

Information Technology

Ricardo Bellucci
Jhones Alves do Nascimento
Júlio Coelho
Matheus Lourenço

Materials and Property

Valdomiro Rodrigues da Silva Neto – *manager*
Larissa Di Ciero Ferradas – *coordinator*
Angélica de Oliveira Divino
Daniel Pereira
Isabela Cardoso
Sergio Faria Lima
Victor Senciel
Vinícius Robson da Silva Araújo
Wagner Pereira de Andrade
Lucas Galhardo – *apprentice*

Planning and Operations

Rone Amabile
Vera Lucia Kogan

Guadeloupe – Dec 5-7, 2024

Lafabri'k – *co-convener*
Marie-Laure Poitout – *partner
 venue presidency*
Léna Blou – *partner venue direction*
Hellen Rugard – *local production*
Annik Benjamin – *simultaneous
 translation*
Cédric Marcellin, Philippe Hurgon –
 *AV content and photographic
 documentation*
Institut Français; Embaixada do
 Brasil em Paris / Instituto
 Guimarães Rosa – Ministério das
 Relações Exteriores – *local support*

Zanzibar – Feb 11-13, 2025

Bernard Ntahondi – *co-convener*
Dhow Countries Music Academy
 (DCMA) – *partner institution*
Halda Alkanaan – *partner institu-
 tion direction*
Thureiya Saleh – *local production*
Raymond Peter, Alex Marcel –
 sound engineering
William Chazega Nkobi,
 Habibu Ramadhani Diliwa – *simul-
 taneous translation*
Aden Rajab Said, Ally Nassor, Arafat
 Khamis Moh'd, Caroline-Jamie
 Dandu, Gulaam Abdullah, Venance
 Leonard, Waleed Khamis
 Mohammed – *AV content and
 photographic documentation*
YAS, Fondation H, Embaixada do
 Brasil em Dar es Salaam / Instituto
 Guimarães Rosa – Ministério das
 Relações Exteriores –
 local support

Tokyo – Apr 12-14, 2025

Andrew Maerkle, Kanako
 Sugiyama – *co-convener*
The 5th Floor; Sogetsu Kaikan;
 The University of Tokyo (with
 ACUT) – *venues*
Jordan A. Y. Smith – *poetry
 program advising*
Tomoya Iwata – *local production*
Yoshiko Kurata – *local press office*
Wataru Shoji – *sound engineering*
Art Translators Collective – *simulta-
 neous translation*
Kenji Agata, Naoki Takehisa, Sora
 Shirai, Takuma Osugi, Yoshikatsu
 Hirayama – *AV content and photo-
 graphic documentation*
Embaixada do Brasil em Tóquio /
 Instituto Guimarães Rosa –
 Ministério das Relações Exteriores;
 Art Center, The University of
 Tokyo (ACUT) – *local support*

The title of the 36th Bienal de São
Paulo, *"Not all travellers walk roads"*,
is made up of verses by writer
Conceição Evaristo.

Educational Publication #2

Edited by
Conceptual team and Fundação
 Bienal de São Paulo

Published by
Fundação Bienal de São Paulo and
 Center for Art, Research and
 Alliances (CARA), in Portuguese
 and English

Design
Studio Yukiko

**Editorial coordination and
graphic production**
Fundação Bienal de São Paulo

Layout
Tamara Lichtenstein

Editorial assistance
Deborah Moreira

Copyediting and proofreading
Bruno Rodrigues, Mariana Nacif
 Mendes, Sandra Brazil

Translation
Ana Laura Borro, Andréia Manfrin,
 Claire Laribe, Jéssica Alonso,
 Philip Somervell

Font families
Arizona and Camera Plain
 by Dinamo

Printing
Ipsis

ISBN
978-1-954939-12-7

Distributed worldwide by
ARTBOOK | D.A.P.
75 Broad Street, Suite 630
New York, NY 10004
orders@dapinc.com
www.artbook.com

Fundação Bienal de São Paulo
Av. Pedro Álvares Cabral – Moema
04094-050 / São Paulo – SP
bienal.org.br

Center for Art, Research and Alliances (CARA)
225 West 13th Street
New York, NY 10011
cara-nyc.org

Cataloging in Publication (CIP)

Bigidi mè pa tonbé: Totter but Never Fall:
      educational publication: vol. 2 /
      edited by Fundação Bienal de São Paulo;
      Bonaventure Soh Bejeng Ndikung. -- São Paulo:
      Bienal de São Paulo, 2025.

ISBN 978-1-954939-12-7

1. Art – São Paulo (State) – Exhibitions
2. Bienal de São Paulo (SP)
3. Culture
4. Education
5. Mediation

I. Fundação Bienal de São Paulo.
II. Ndikung, Bonaventure Soh Bejeng.

25-273124   CDD-709.8161

Systematic Catalog Index:
Art Biennials: São Paulo: City 709.8161

Marcele Souto – Librarian – CRB-8/9241

Notes

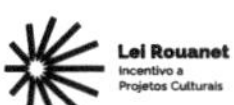

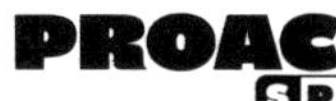

strategic partnership

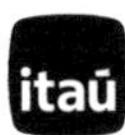

master sponsorship

Bloomberg   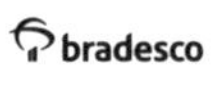   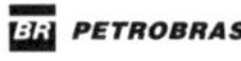   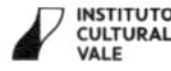   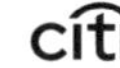   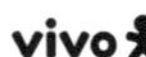

sponsorship

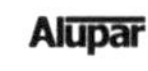   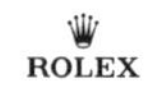      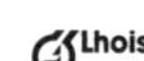

OSKLEN   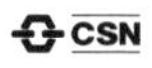   comgas   MATTOS FILHO   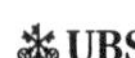

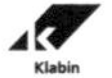   Unipar   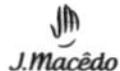   

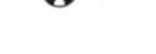   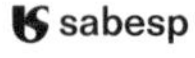   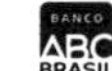   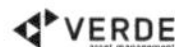   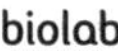

official carrier   official agency   support

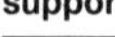    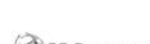   

cultural partnership

                    J.P.Morgan   

international support

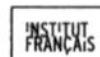   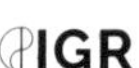      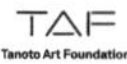   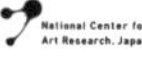

local support   local partnership

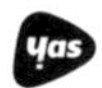   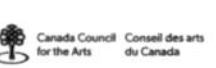   

institutional support   realization

   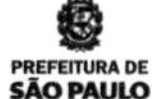   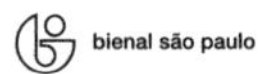   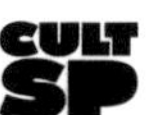   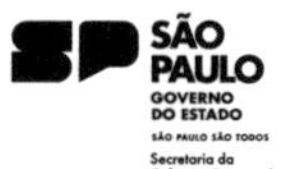   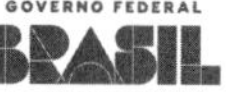